Building Your Perfect Bike

BUILDING YOUR PERFECT BIKE

From Bare Frame to Personalized Superbike

Richard Ries

Photographs by the author except as credited

BICYCLE BOOKS

FROM

Motorbooks International
Publishers & Wholesalers ®

First published in 1997 by Motorbooks International Publishers & Wholesalers, 729 Prospect Avenue, PO Box 1, Osceola, WI 54020-0001 USA

Motorbooks International is a certified trademark, registered with the United States Patent Office

The information in this book is true and complete to the best of our knowledge. All recommendations are made without any guarantee on the part of the author or Publisher, who also disclaim any liability incurred in connection with the use of this data or specific details

We recognize that some words, model names and designations, for example, mentioned herein are the property of the trademark holder. We use them for identification purposes only. This is not an official publication

Motorbooks International books are also available at discounts in bulk quantity for industrial or sales-promotional use. For details write to Special Sales Manager at the Publisher's address

Library of Congress Cataloging-in-Publication Data
Ries, Richard R.
    Building Your Perfect Bike: Specifying and equipping the right bike for your personal use.
        Includes index.
    1. Bicycles and bicycling—manuals, handbooks, etc. 2. Authorship. I. Title
LC Catalogue
Card Number 96-84655
ISBN 0-933201-77-X

On the front cover: A Crosstrac full-suspension frame provided the basis for one of the project bikes built for this book. *Richard Ries*
Detail photos, top to bottom: Rear end of a rigid-frame mountain bike based on an Ibis frame equipped with Shimano Deore XT derailleur. *Neil van der Plas*
Spinergy's RevRok 4-bladed downhill mountain bike wheel. *Richard Ries*
Grafton cantilever brakes with Mojo brake cable hanger on a full-suspension mountain bike. *Richard Ries*
Shimano XT derailleur and chainrings on a Ritchie hardtail mountain bike. *Gene Anthony*

On the back cover: High-end Campagnolo road bike gruppo. *Photo courtesy Campagnolo*

Printed in Hong Kong

To Julie, with thanks for believing
and
to Betty, with thanks for everything

Richard Ries got his first bicycle on his sixth birthday in November of 1959. It was a single-speed Western Flyer from a Western Auto store, and he was in heaven. Since then, he's never been without a bike for more than a few months at a time. From the Western Flyer he graduated to a Schwinn 2-speed and then to a series of 10-speeds.

"I've always loved the engineering that goes into bicycles," says Ries. "I could pore over an 1890s Columbia tandem tricycle for hours." Modern engineering, including exotic frame materials, wheel design, and electronics, are equally fascinating to him.

A freelance writer since 1986, Ries shifted his focus in the early 1990s to consumer bicycle magazines. His articles have appeared in *Bike, Bicycling, MTB, Dirt Rag, Bicycle Guide,* and other magazines before he undertook this project.

Never a racer, Ries has always been a recreational rider. He logs about 5,000 miles per year. Roughly 80 percent of those are road miles, the rest done on a mountain bike.

Ries is an honor graduate of Indiana University Southeast with a B.A. in English. He lives in Madison, Indiana, with his wife and stepson. "We think about moving sometimes," he says, "but then I go ride the hills and hollows that lie right outside my back door and realize this is as close to perfect riding as I'm likely to find."

Table of Contents

Author
Richard Ries
riding one of
the completed
project bikes.

Chapter 1

What This Book Is All About

The purpose of this book is threefold. First, I hope to help you realize the scope of what's available. There are millions of parts out there from thousands of manufacturers, running the gamut from tiny operations of one man or woman in a garage to multimillion-dollar, multinational corporations like Shimano.

Second, I hope to help you imagine your personal perfect bike. In bike building, as in most things, some decisions are more important than others. Knowing what's available only helps if you know what you need.

Third, I hope to show how you can build your personal dream bike. There's nothing on a bike that a rider of average mechanical ability can't handle. But the sequence and method of assembly are important, and there are a lot of tips on specific bicycles and components. That's the type of information found in this book.

What's the Difference? No other book available to date looks at bike building the way this one does. Others may say how to install or adjust a part, but not how to select that part in the first place. Nor do other books take the long view of integrating parts and rider into one harmonious unit.

And that's really what you want. Your bike should be an extension of you. Not just physically, but spiritually as well. It should reflect your values, your ideals. Do you have a need for speed? Do you value tradition? If you have to choose between performance and appearance, which will it be? Should your bike be a rolling shrine of high technology, or of efficient transportation?

This is not a mechanical handbook. The concepts given here can be applied to any number of specific products, yet there are far too many special applications and unique operations for them all to be included here. Besides, there's no sense duplicating the efforts of others.

Several good how-to books already exist. You will need one of those books. I suppose you could blunder your way into an assembled bike without one, but why? In order of usefulness, here are the sources you should consider:

1. The instructions that come with the parts. No one knows their parts like the manufacturers do, so read and follow closely their instructions. Regrettably, at times it seems creating the instructions was the most challenging aspect of creating a part. Many instructions are poorly written or poorly illustrated, or simply don't make sense. If you can't decide between two similar parts, the quality of the instructions may be a good deciding factor. Worst offenders are often the small manufacturers of components,

Photo 1-1

The first project bike was this road bike based on a SoftRide Beam frame. With Paris-Roubaix front suspension and Spinergy 4-bladed wheels, it is fast and comfortable. Not light, though.

Photo 1-2

The second project bike was this road touring bike based on a custom-built frame by California frame builder Bernie Mikkelsen. Built specifically to meet the rider's sound, though seemingly idiosyncratic, ideas about how a touring bike should be, it sports a range of relatively common parts, in addition to a full range of touring accessories.

although even the big dogs can leave you scratching your head at times.

2. A standard bicycle repair manual, such as Rob van der Plas's *Bicycle Repair Book, Mountain Bike Maintenance,* or *Road Bike Maintenance.* To help you understand how components work, his *Bicycle Technology* is another good source of information.

3. *Bicycling Magazine's Complete Guide to Bicycle Maintenance and Repair* covers most things well, has clear illustrations, and is nicely arranged. It has information on such archaic applications as cottered cranks as well as newer concepts, such as rear suspension designs.

4. *The Haynes Bicycle Book* is a good resource from a company that has for many years done an excellent job with motor vehicle maintenance books, who have now expanded to the field of bicycles as well.

5. *Sutherland's Handbook for Bicycle Mechanics* is the classic tome from Howard Sutherland, et al. Sold in the form of a ring binder, this is the industry's bible of shape, size, fit, and other minutiae. Not a necessity, but if you ever get about $125 ahead, it should be the first luxury item on your bookshelf.

The Projects In this book, the process of building up your perfect bike — a different bike for everyone — is demonstrated and illustrated by following the three projects I accomplished myself for this purpose: a full-suspension mountain bike, a sophisticated road bike, and a

Photo 1-3

The third project bike was going to be built first — it just took that much longer to come together. Based on the quite spectacular Crosstrack suspension frame, all registers had to be pulled to tune it. The result, though, is agreat full-suspension mountain bike.

special touring bike based on a custom-designed frame. In addition, I will cover in less detail the subject of special problems encountered on a tandem, based on a custom-designed frame.

All three specially built-up bikes finished up being excellent machines, reflecting my choices. But this is not to say any other configuration — different frame, different components — would not have yielded bikes that are more suitable for other riders and builders. Look at these projects, not as the answers to the quest for "your perfect bike," but as examples to illustrate how to go about the process of defining and building it.

There's not a component in here that I wouldn't recommend to someone else. The fact that a certain set of brakes or a specific crankset found its way onto a project bike, while another did not, is no statement of the relative merits of the individual models. There's really only room for one of each part on any one bike, and sometimes the decision was based on available size — crank-arm length or stem diameter, for example. In other cases it was based on color or some other personal but trivial preference. Again, these are all quality products. After all, if you're building your perfect bike, you don't let in junk parts.

About the Photos

The illustrations used in this book are workshop shots showing the work as it was actually progressing. No doubt, prettier photos could have been taken in a photo studio — but not more realistic ones.

I worked on the bikes outdoors, and that's where the photos were taken. Consequently, there are variations in shadows and lighting depending on the season, the time of day, and the weather. If nothing else, these photos make a statement: bikes and the people working on them belong outdoors, not cooped up under artificial lights.

The Ride's the Thing

A short ride on a bad bike is better than no ride at all. But a great ride on a perfect bike is nirvana.

This book is for all of you who, like me, stare in wonder at the engineering and design that go into so humble a vehicle. It's for everyone that still gets a jump start of adrenalin from the first revolution of the cranks on every ride.

If, like Sisyphus, you were condemned to do one thing for eternity, and if (unlike Sisyphus) you could chose that thing, and you'd chose riding a bike of your own creation — this is your book.

Chapter 2

Before You Build

Building the perfect anything starts with developing the perfect plan. That's as true for a bicycle as it is for a house, a piece of machinery, or a garden. So get out paper and pencil, and soon we'll begin planning. But planning for what? What will your bike do? Bicycles come in an unbelievable variety. What will yours be like?

We'll start our planning process in a minute. But first, to appreciate how complex and how refined our planning must be, let's look at an analogy.

Of Hammers and Bicycles

Of all the tools on earth, a hammer is perhaps the simplest. Yet walk into any hardware store, and you'll see dozens of different hammers on display. There are framing hammers, sledgehammers, machinists' hammers, and geologists' hammers. There are hammers with heads made of steel, brass, plastic, and rubber. There are short-handled hammers and long-handled hammers.

Why so many hammers? Because there are so many intended uses for them. You could drive a nail with a sledgehammer, but it wouldn't be your first choice. You could break rock with a jeweler's hammer, but you'd have to be awfully patient.

Selecting the right hammer relies on asking the right question: What will you use it for? That same question is where we start planning your perfect bike.

What Do You Need?

Defining your needs will define your bike. Where will you be riding? What do you expect to do with the bike? What kind of budget are you working with?

Some needs are determined, not by the environment in which you ride, but by your own qualities. Any extreme requires extra thought. Are you taller, shorter, lighter, or heavier than average? Are your legs long for your height? Are your legs of equal length? Do you have any medical conditions — carpal tunnel syndrome, chondromalacia, or a bad back — that will have to be taken into consideration?

The more closely you define your needs, the more closely your bike will match them. You can build a perfect bike for time trials, track races, club centuries, touring, commuting, fitness, downhill,

**Photo 2-1:
Project Bike No. 1
Road Bike**

The SoftRide Power V frame is a carbon fiber monocoque design. The interior of the frame is foam filled to reduce harmonic vibration on the road.

SoftRide's philosophy is to suspend the rider, not the bike. Their beam bikes are available in carbon fiber, aluminum, and steel, in road, mountain, and touring styles. The beam is also available as a kit to retrofit to other bikes.

SoftRide also offers a suspension stem, which was used on the Mikkelsen touring bike. For front suspension here, a Rock Shox Paris-

Roubaix road fork was used. The Paris-Roubaix fork is air-sprung and oil-damped. Atop each fork leg is a dial that alters the damping rate. Setting number 1 is plushest, number 6 is locked out.

Chris King provided the headset. King headsets are known for their indestructibility and jewelry store–quality finish. This Team model followed the tradition. Even though loosening was never a problem on earlier models, newer ones have an improved lockring and thread collet.

The Paris-Roubaix fork is lighter than other suspension fork styles, but is still 1 to 1½ lb. heavier than

a quality rigid fork, such as the Kinesis aluminum model supplied with the SoftRide frame. The Kinesis fork provides a fairly supple ride, but I wanted a true full-suspension road bike.

Also upping the total weight are the Spinergy wheels. Compared to standard spoked wheels, the Spinergy wheels add about 1 lb. to the bike. The difference is even greater when compared to minimalist wheels, such as the Cronometro.

The other bad news on the Spinergy wheels: they're much more skitterish in crosswinds than traditional spoked wheels.

The good news: their aerodynamic benefit becomes apparent at speed. They are fast, fast, fast wheels. Although their weight holds down their acceleration, their carbon fiber blades stir the air very little once up to speed. The difference at speeds above 20 mph was especially apparent.

The other good news: they're comfortable wheels that are also very rigid.

Holding the wheels in place are Salsa Flip-Off skewers. They're light, strong, and beautiful. Best of all, they come from Ross Shafer, who's perfectly happy to remain a free thinker in

an industry that's becoming increasingly corporate.

The component group on this bike is all Sachs New Record. It's really Campy equipment with a different nameplate, and behaves much like any other Campy I've ridden. Brakes are powerful, controls are intuitive, and the shifting, which was finicky at first, got smoother and more positive as the miles piled on.

Mating the Sachs rear derailleur to the Shimano-compatible hub was accomplished with a spacer kit from Wheels Manufacturing. The shifting never attained the crispness of an all-Sachs or all-Shimano system, but it was still very good. Wheels Manufacturing produces a stunning array of gewgaws and tidbits, all beautifully machined and exquisitely finished. Ordering their catalog is worthwhile just to look at all the goodies they offer. It's almost as if elves were running the place.

The bike is shod with Vittoria Open Corsa CX tires and Vittoria latex tubes. The ride was promised to be almost indistinguishable from sew-ups. Not so. But they're fine tires nonetheless. Ride quality is very good. Puncture resistance is excellent. Cornering is nothing short of awesome. The

latex tubes were another story. The first one lasted less than 10 miles; the other made it to almost 100.

The saddle is a Terry TFI. Georgeanne Terry made such a name for herself crafting women's cycling goodies — from clothes to saddles to complete bikes — that she was afraid her line of men's accessories wouldn't be accepted if it sported the Terry name, so TFI was born.

The saddle is narrow but extremely comfortable. The center section is designed to alleviate pressure on the prostate gland and the penile nerves. It seems to work. The saddle is lightweight. My only complaint is the same one I have about all chisel-nosed saddles: they tend to snag the crotch of my shorts when I go from standing to sitting.

The handlebars are a mix. The drops are Profile; the aero bars are Scott. I could have gone with all Scott or all Profile, but this was the combination that fit me best.

(continued on page 15)

(continued from page 14)

I've had good luck with Scott bars before. I've racked up several thousand miles on AT-4 Pro bars on one of my mountain bikes and on drop handlebars on one of my road bikes with absolutely no problem. So I was disappointed to find that one of the clamps for these aero bars had badly damaged threads. I was also surprised when the nylon cover peeled back on one of the armrests within the first 10 miles. My experience tells me this was a fluke, not a new direction in quality control at Scott. At least I hope so.

The bars are wrapped with Off the Front tape. I love Off the Front for their wild designs, but also for the quality of their tape. It's cushioned just enough, has no sticky adhesive backing, and washes up nicely.

Off the Front also provided the rubber pads that smooth out the contour of the hooks on these bars. The pads spread the contact from the edges of your hands all the way across the palms to reduce fatigue and improve control.

single-track, or stage racing, but you can't build one bike that will do all of those things. This doesn't mean your touring bike can't be used for commuting, or that your downhill bike can't be used for a run to the grocery store.

Just remember that bike design lies on a continuum. If "track bike" is at one end and "commuter" is on the other, the middle ground will be a bike that does neither well. The closer you move to either end, the better the bike will perform that duty and the worse it will do the other.

Have a Fit

So you've decided this bike will be built for long rides. You'll be doing lots of centuries, many on poorly maintained secondary roads. The bike will have to be light but sturdy, and comfortable in

Photo 2-2

My goal was to build a fast, comfortable

bike suitable for century rides on the poorly maintained roads near my rural home. Did I succeed? Yes and no.

The bike is comfortable and fast. It's also heavy. Switching to a rigid fork and Cronometro wheels would save several pounds, a noticeable difference when climbing or sprinting. Further weight loss could be had by swapping the heavy bottom bracket supplied by Sachs for a lighter model.

Would the change be worthwhile? Probably. I'm a lousy climber anyway, and I need every advantage to stay with the group on club rides in hilly terrain. On the other hand, the bike performs well now, and the comfort would be hard to forsake in the name of climbing speed.

In the end, I decided to keep the bike as it is. If it becomes necessary to replace a part, I'll look for weight savings then. For now I'm happy with a bike that rides like a lounge chair, corners like a roller coaster, descends like a meteor, even though it climbs like a brick.

demanding conditions. You're ready to start ordering parts, right?

Not quite. Let's return to the hammer analogy for just a minute. You've been shopping for a hammer. You need it to do some general carpentry, including framing. You've settled on an Estwing straight-claw model with the blue rubber grip, and you're ready to buy.

But wait. Before you can plunk down your money, you have to decide what size you need. A 16 oz. hammer doesn't pack the punch of its bigger brothers, so it takes longer to do the job. On the other hand, even a gorilla would get tired after a day of swinging the 28 oz. model. You settle for the middle ground, a 22 oz. beauty that feels just right when you pick it up. You have found the perfect fit.

The Right Size   If fit is critical to our simplest tools, it must surely be as important to something as complex as a bicycle. The first time I rode on the Major Taylor velodrome in Indianapolis, I couldn't find a bike in my size, so I ended up riding one 5 cm too small. The result? My quadriceps were on fire, my lap times were pitiful, and I could barely draw in enough air to keep from blacking out.

A friend searched deeper into the stockpile of bikes and discovered a larger frame. When he was done with it, I got off the one I'd been using and got onto his. The difference was dramatic. I was instantly more comfortable and faster, and I felt as though I could ride forever.

The finest bike in the world would be completely worthless to you if it didn't fit right. There is no other single element that will affect the joy you derive from the finished product more than the way it fits you. Every dimension must be correct.

If the chainstays are too short on your touring bike, your heels will clip the panniers on every revolution. That's not touring; that's torture. If the top tube is too long on your road bike, your wrists, arms, shoulders, and back will be in agony before your legs are even warmed up. If the stem is too short on your mountain bike, you'll never keep the front wheel planted while climbing.

How do you determine the proper fit? Start with the bike you're riding now. What feels right? What needs to be changed?

Shops and builders offer fit services. Sometimes that involves merely plugging your body dimensions into a formula. A better approach is to use one of the machines, such as the Fit Kit, designed for the purpose.

The best solution comes from Bernie Mikkelsen, the builder who provided the touring frame for this book. Bernie has created a bicycle frame for which every dimension is adjustable. Want to know what another inch in the top tube feels like? Curious about the effects of another half a degree of head angle? With a twist of the wrench, Bernie can provide that. He makes the adjustment, you ride a bit, then you can try something else. It's the most clever, effective fit tool available today.

Enlightened shops are using Mikkelsen's adjustable bike. Call around until you find one, or call Bernie and ask him where the nearest dealer is located.

No Time to Be Proud

When designing your bike, remember you're not a pioneer. Others have gone before you. Even Graeme Obree, whose bikes were hailed as revolutionary in the early 1990s, didn't stray far from traditional design in his creations. Yes, using parts from a washing machine to build a bottom bracket was a little odd, but the whole bike still looked like a bike.

If you lived in Salt Lake City and had to drive to Omaha, you wouldn't set out with a tank of gas, a compass, and a hopeful look on your face. You'd consult maps to find the best route. You'd rely on transportation experts to provide you with the information you needed to complete your journey quickly, safely, and economically.

The experts you need now are the product manufacturers. Although sometimes taken to task in the bicycle press for coming up with a seemingly endless variety of designs, these manufacturers are constantly improving their products through research and testing. Changes aren't made on a whim; they reflect a purposeful move toward a better product. Tell a manufacturer what you have in mind — you're likely to get a product that fits the need.

Perhaps more than anyone else in the business, frame builders are fanatical about design. Most are consumed by their occupation. No subtlety of design, no nuance of tubing performance escapes their attention. They are a unique mix of old-world craftsmanship and new-age technology.

Other experts hang out at your local bike shop, cleverly disguised as employees and customers. Employees see a constant parade of parts from dozens of manufacturers. They see these parts on customers' bikes and their own. They know what works and what doesn't.

Customers also know what works. Pay attention to what other people are riding. Ask them what they like and dislike about the products they use.

If you're fortunate enough to have a good shop in your area, don't hesitate to use the people there for information and service. Cultivate a good relationship with them now, so they'll be there when you need them. How? Ask intelligent questions. Respect their opinions. Most of all, buy what you can from them. These shops are not libraries, supported with government subsidies so they can dispense information for free. They rely on customers to stay alive.

You're the Judge Remember, however, that the bike you're building is your own. If the shop employees offer advice that doesn't ring true, or if they try to convince you to buy a part you know doesn't meet your standards, go elsewhere. You'll be riding your bike long after they've dumped their white elephants on some other unsuspecting person.

The quality of your final product depends in large part on your willingness to pick the brains of others. They will help you define your needs, select parts, and avoid pitfalls.

You may think you know everything you need to know about building your perfect bicycle. You'd be wrong. This is no time to be proud. Manufacturers have millions of dollars invested in research and design, and it's all available to you if you ask. Shops and other riders have invested time and money in evaluating components. Their accumulated wisdom makes a good starting point for your project.

Photo 2-3

The heart of the SoftRide's rear suspension is the beam that attaches at the front to a pivot bolt. The hex-head nut tightens an Allen bolt. Loosening this bolt allows the beam to be pivoted up or down to adjust effective seat height. A little adjustment at the front yields a large change at the saddle, so SoftRide is able to offer just three frame sizes to fit a broad range of rider height.

Not everyone in this business is equally capable of helping you, nor equally willing to do so. Sometimes a person's ego intrudes; sometimes he or she just doesn't know the answer. Call around until you find someone with whom you're comfortable. The time you spend now will be paid back exponentially later, when you're riding.

Can You Spell "Frustration"?

The good news is that the world's full of experts. The bad news is that even they sometimes fall down. Why? Because all this designing often seems to occur in a vacuum. If ever there were an industry in desperate need of standardization, it is cycling.

It's not just seatpost sizes or bottom bracket spindle lengths. It's little things, unexpected things.

Example number one: the Mikkelsen touring bike here has a 1 in. headset. I installed a Dia-Compe Thread Head headset. I measured the stack height and cut the fork to fit.

Photo 2-4

The goal in building this bike was to have something suitable for a wide variety of riding chores. It could go on long club rides, quick trips to the store, or extended tours.

Complicating this goal were the owner's requirements. She wanted a bike that mimicked the geometry of another of her bikes, right down to the sloping top tube. Unlike that other bike, however, this one would have to be light and possess good all-day road manners.

Frame builder Bernie Mikkelsen worked with the rider to develop this frame. Was it a success? Yes, although as of this writing the owner hasn't had a chance for an extended tour.

Problems encountered involved mostly the Shimano 105 triple chainrings and the 105 STI controls. After several exchanges of incorrect parts, the correct levers finally arrived. They were indexed for a triple — but not this triple. Jumps could be made between two rings — small and middle or middle and big — but not across all three. It took endless fiddling and a series of calls to Shimano to finally get things working right.

The wheels are Mavic T217 36-hole touring rims laced to TNT hubs with DT Swiss 14-gauge stainless steel spokes. The wheels are retained with Kore quick releases. Vittoria Tecno Twin Tread tires in 700C x 28 provide minimal rolling resistance and excellent cornering adhesion.

Terry handlebars are attached to a SoftRide suspension stem and are wrapped in Off the Front tape. The fork, like the frame, was custom-built by Bernie Mikkelsen. A Shimano 600 headset was used.

The 170 mm crank, both derailleurs, and the STI controls are all Shimano 105. American Classic provided the bottom bracket. Brakes are Paul Stoplights MC.

A Terry saddle is attached to a Shimano XTR seatpost. Pedals are Shimano M323 with a platform on one side and SPD cleats on the other.

The problem arose when I tried to install the front brake cable hanger. A lip on the crown nut of the headset, which had to fit into the bearing, prevented the use of the hanger. I tried other headsets, but none had the right stack height with the hanger in place. In the end, I had to send the fork back to Bernie. He welded on an extension — exquisite work, by the way — so that I could get the correct steerer tube length. (He also provided the turned aluminum spacer between the headset nut and top bearing.)

Example number two: I had hoped to use the Shimano V-brakes on the Crosstrac Sonoma. Their stopping power and off-center cable routing were attractive features. But because of the Crosstrac's unusual frame and fork design, the brakes wouldn't work.

My next choice was to use the V-brakes on the Mikkelsen touring bike. They could be made to work in back, but they wouldn't open up far enough to allow tire changes in front; the pads hit the fork legs. Rather than run two types of brakes on one bike, I put the V-brakes aside for another project.

Special Parts, Special Tools

The problems aren't over when you're done building. Unique parts require unique tools to service them. One of my older mountain bikes requires at least a half-dozen Allen wrenches for trailside repair. The 5 and 6 mm fit bottle cage bolts, derailleur clamps, and other standard parts. But I also need a 2 mm for the bottom bracket, a $5/16$in. for the lockring on the headset, a 2.5 mm for the barrel bolts that secure the brake cables — the list goes on.

Example number three: After trying two different derailleurs on the Crosstrac, I was convinced the frame was somehow defective. At the bottom of its mounting tube, the derailleur still hung 2 in. above the chainrings, whereas this distance is supposed to be only 1 to 3 mm.

Then I compared the derailleurs to an older XT model on one of my other bikes. I discovered that Shimano had changed the design. Where the old derailleur's cage was 1 in. below the mounting clamp, the new styles were ½ in. *above* the clamp. On a traditional frame with a continuous seat tube, this wouldn't matter. But on the Crosstrac's abbreviated derailleur mounting stub, the new styles couldn't be made to work. The solution? I shopped around until I found an old LX derailleur.

The moral of this story? There are two. First, don't assume any part will work, no matter how "standard" it appears, until you've tried it yourself. Second, weigh the "gee-whiz" factor of any new component against the headache of maintaining unusual or overly complex parts.

Helping make sense of the hodgepodge of sizes and styles is Howard Sutherland, et al. *Sutherland's Handbook for Bicycle Mechanics* is several hundred pages of specifications and diagrams that take most of the mystery out of what fits what. It's expensive (the 1996 edition retailed for $125), and because it's targeted toward professional mechanics, it can leave amateur mechanics scratching their heads at times. But it's a gold mine of information. If you can't afford one of your own, make friends with a shop that has one.

Prioritize Your Pennies

Remember when American Bicycle Manufacturing came up with their $25,000 beryllium frame? For the purposes of this book, we can look at that frame and deduce two important points.

First, there's virtually no limit to how much you can spend on a bicycle. Second, because the frame was later stolen, it reminds us that our finished product deserves the best security. Stealing a purchased bike is theft. Stealing one that the owner *built* is kidnaping.

Back to the first point. Decide now what your budget will be. Don't just have a figure in mind. Write it down. Then make your parts fit within that budget. Better yet, make them fit with about 10 percent to spare. You'll find places to spend that cushion as the project progresses.

How do you allocate your budget? There are no rules, but you can try a 50-40-10 split. Spend 50 percent on the drivetrain and wheels, 40 percent on the frame, and 10 percent on everything else. That ratio will change depending on the type of bike you're building. For example, "everything else" on a touring bike may be 30 percent of the total cost; on a tandem, the frame may be 60 percent of the total.

Within the budget, but separate from the bike itself, will be tools and supplies, such as grease. Tools likely to see frequent future use, or those that are inexpensive, are worthwhile investments. Examples would include cone wrenches, spoke wrenches, and bottom bracket tools.

Some tools are hard to justify because they're expensive and infrequently used. Examples here would include a headset bearing press and spoke tensiometer. The jobs for which these tools are required may be accomplished more economically by taking the bike to a shop rather than purchasing the tool.

Photos 2-5, 2-6, 2-7

It's three o'clock in the morning. I'm sitting on the kitchen floor working on this bike, and my editor needed to have the write-up on it a month ago. I'm on the verge of tears.

I'm drilling holes in parts of this frame, specifically, the bracket that supports the front derailleur. I'm thinking this may be a bad idea. This may weaken something. It may lead to failure of some part on the trail.

Big deal. Right now, I'd welcome that. If this whole thing folded up underneath me, I could take it to the recyclers, where it could be made into something useful. At least it would be out of my life.

The problems didn't start until I opened the box — just a few short months after the supplier had assured me I would have it. I had been promised a frame in a dazzling shade of red. Instead, it was a color best described as godawful orange. Worse yet, it was peppered with decals. On the upside, it gave me an opportunity to demonstrate how to repaint a frame (see Chapter 3).

Next up: the seatpost. It's a proprietary design (good luck finding a replacement if you wreck this one), made to accommodate the wide range of seat tube angles this frame provides. That much it does very well. Unfortunately, adapting it to the TFI saddle took an entire morning.

Shimano's V-brakes wouldn't work with the strange backwards fork brace. The rear dropouts had to be filed down before they'd accept a hub — any hub. The front dropouts had such deep "lawyer recesses" (wheel hub retention devices) that I had to completely remove the knurled end of the skewer to free the wheel, which resulted in the immediate loss of one of the conical springs from the skewer.

Then there was that front derailleur. Shimano changed the design of their derailleurs in midstream, effectively moving the cage 2 in. higher relative to the band clamp. The Shimano XT model Crosstrac I had specified hung 'way above the chainrings. I found an old LX derailleur that would fit, but I couldn't make it shift.

After a flurry of phone calls, faxes, and messages to Fred Saldena at Strom Industries — Crosstrac's distributor — I was no closer than I was before.

I went back to the skimpy instruction manual and found item 17, which said in part: "Replace the cable clamp bolt with the trunion bolt that is provided with your assembly package." There was no trunion bolt; there was no assembly package.

You'd think the problem with the derailleur or the missing part would have occurred to someone at Strom, especially considering I had specifically requested a fax showing cable routing and had explained that something seemed to be missing. But that never happened.

In the end I jury-rigged my own routing, which coupled with a $2 pulley and an S-hook from the hardware store, did the trick. The pulley was attached to a bolt in the bottom bracket shell that Crosstrac had provided but which seemed to have no function. I was drilling holes for this cable routing at the beginning of this saga.

The only thing that could redeem this whole miserable experience was a great ride. Guess what: I got it.

(continued on page 23)

(continued from page 22)

The Sonoma is what a full-suspension bike should be. Handling is precise. Weight is higher than that of a high-end bike with front suspension only, but it is well balanced and rarely objectionable. The ride is sublime.

The bike floats over anything in its path. Spring rates are excellent, and damping is at least very good. Rebound damping on both ends seemed a little light. On the other hand, neither the shock nor the fork packed up on stutter bumps.

Drawbacks found on other full-suspension bikes were minimized on the Crosstrac. To give an example, pedal-induced suspension action was acceptably low in all three chainrings. The most pronounced full-suspension trait was that, with the brakes applied, the back end would lift quite a bit. It didn't take long to learn to compensate for that by shifting more weight to the rear when braking.

Why did the Crosstrac work so well in the end? First of all because of good design. The frame, fork, and Fox shock, all provided by Crosstrac, worked very well together.

The second reason was the right choice of components. The 1¼ in. Dia-Compe threadless headset (also provided by Crosstrac) held a Control Tech stem, which in turn held Salsa's Go Moto handlebars and Scott bar-ends. On the bars were Grip Shift X-Ray shifters and grips.

Grafton brakes and levers worked beautifully front and rear. The front brake's odd factory linkage resulted in a spongy feel. The back brake was much more positive. Note the Ringlé Mojo cable hanger — function and form in unison.

Cronometro wheels were light and fast, but the pinging of the spokes as they bedded in under a 200 lb. rider was a bit unnerving. As of this writing, the wheels have very few miles on them, and they're still pinging, but have not shown any cause for concern.

The Wilderness Trail Bike Veloci-Raptor tires worked well in a surprising range of conditions: grassy slopes, rocky creek beds, and dry hardpack trails.

The Cook Brothers E cranks and Ritchey WCS pedals worked wonderfully, as did the Carnac Dune shoes, Shimano XT rear and LX front derailleurs, and SDG Kevlar saddle.

I used Slick Whips cables from Talon Cycles. These are coated with PTFE (better known by its most common brand name, Teflon). The low-friction, low-maintenance cables dramatically improve braking and shifting. They use standard housing but require special ferrules, which are available in an anodized finish.

Did the ride quality make up for everything else? Not quite. Building a bike should not have to involve this much frustration. And getting help should not always require waiting for someone to check voice mail before getting back to you. It would have been nice to have a human voice answer the phone at Strom occasionally.

But some day, riding on cloud nine, I may forget all that.

Should you never buy an expensive tool? That depends on four things. One, the likelihood you'll use that tool again. It doesn't take too many headsets to justify the cost of the bearing press. Two, how adamant you are about doing all the work yourself. Three, how convenient it is to have someone else do those jobs. For example, from where I live, it's an hour to the nearest shop with a bearing press. And four, whether the task can be completed with another, more common tool or technique.

Supplies are less of a problem. Although it's good to use bicycle-specific products, in most cases it's not necessary. For example, any water-resistant grease can be used on bearings. (The exception is chain lube. Nothing is an acceptable substitute for the right stuff on chains.)

Where to Spend Bicycles are the gestalt approach to transportation and recreation: the whole is far greater than the sum of its parts. Still, some parts are worth more than others.

As you're prioritizing your resources, your first concern should be with the frame. No other part will make as big a difference in the quality of the riding experience. Nor will any other part last as long. A good frame, well maintained, will endure for your lifetime. It will outlast dozens of rims and hubs and derailleurs.

After the frame, the next most important consideration is the wheels. A good wheel is light, so it accelerates quickly. It's also durable, so it resists impact damage and stays true with little attention. It also has a good ride quality, being at once comfortable and precise.

Next in line is the drivetrain. A great frame and responsive wheels are small comfort if every other shift is missed or if braking is accompanied by prayer. The good news is that virtually all modern components offer excellent performance.

The risk comes when you mix and match. Some combinations improve performance; others degrade it. It's safest to go with a drivetrain all from one manufacturer, but that also limits your creativity and may not deliver the performance you seek. Ask around; remember the sources we already discussed.

The main points of contact between you and your bike require some thought, too. Your body weight will be suspended for hours at a time on three very small contact areas: the palms of your hands, a few square inches of butt and inner thigh, and a small area on the soles of your feet. Make sure these areas are comfortable, or your whole body will ache.

Finally, give some thought to accessories. This is most complex with larger items, such as panniers, but even small things matter. Does the computer have the functions you want? Will the cages hold water bottles securely, but still release them when you need a drink?

You'll notice that these items are listed in the order in which you'd likely be willing to change things if necessary after your bike is built. Swapping bottles cages would be no big deal, but changing frames would have you looking into golf or fly fishing.

Where to Save   One of the nice things about building your own bike is that you can squirrel away parts as you encounter them on sale. For example, I was once in a shop in Minneapolis where there was a wall full of name-brand frames — your choice, $99 each. Some even had headsets and bottom brackets. They were all new. The shop got them on a buyout somewhere.

Watch for bargains on components when the new ones come out. You may find last year's highest-rated gruppo for 50 percent off when this year's parts hit the shelf. These specials are getting harder to find, though, as manufacturers get better at inventory control. In fact, you're more likely to find shortages of popular parts in mid-year than you are to find leftovers at the end of the year.

Closeouts and discontinued items can also be found at deeply discounted prices. One dealer I know in Indiana bought up some SunTour hubs when that company ceased operations in the United States, and was selling them at half their original cost.

There are dangers in buying ahead, though. The biggest is the risk that what you buy won't work on what you build. Some parts, such as seatposts, are hopelessly nonstandard. Even standard parts, such as hubs and bottom brackets, can be tricky. It's best to have your complete plan in mind when you buy any individual parts.

Be Flexible   When I conceived this book, it was my intention to take a "rifle" approach to securing products. I would zero in on one manufacturer and try to get parts there. It seemed appropriate to offer each one an exclusive spot in the book, even though there are dozens and even hundreds of manufacturers of any given bike part.

The months went by. Manufacturer promises piled up, but the products did not. My original deadline came and went, and I was still far short of the parts I needed to complete these bikes.

To save my sanity and this book, I switched from a rifle to a shotgun. I contacted dozens of suppliers in hopes that one of them would follow through on its promises. Four months later, I was ready to begin assembling bikes and shooting photos.

What's the moral for you? Simply this: don't be so set on any one item that your whole project is thrown into jeopardy if it's not available. Manufacturers are constantly juggling a million demands, and keeping product in the pipeline can be a problem for them. In the midst of designing new items, planning for trade shows,

Photo 2-8
Although not built specifically for this book, you'll also hear about this tandem.

Like the touring bike, it is based on a frame by California frame builder Bernie Mikkelsen, who also buit the touring bike frame. The owners wanted a fast but comfortable and maneuverable road tandem, and that's what they got. Equipped with Ritchie tandem crankset, Sanshin bolt-on tandem hubs, and Mavic 48-hole rims, the only weak spot is the braking, and they're still working on that without necessarily adding the rear drum brake that could be mounted. (Both the frame and the rear hub are designed for this proven tandem brake configuration if necessary.)

(photo: Neil van der Plas)

sponsoring race teams, cultivating personnel, calculating marketing strategies, and remaining solvent, shortages sometimes occur.

An added benefit of my midstream change of course is that you'll have the opportunity to see how different manufacturers approach the same part. Every item in this book has some unique feature to recommend it. Whether that feature is important to you is your call.

Each section describes the selection process for the parts it contains. Product features are matched with their benefits to the rider. Any pertinent caveats are discussed as well. Benefits are specific to the products shown, but because product life in the bicycle industry is notoriously short, benefits are described in generic terms, too. If you can't find the exact model shown here, you should at least be able to apply the guidelines to select something similar.

It's important to note that in most cases the components selected when assembling a certain bike aren't necessarily better or worse than the others shown. Oftentimes the selection was by whim. Sometimes, it was because the features of an item more closely matched the rider's personal needs. Sometimes it was an issue of size: either how the part fit the bike (seatposts) or how the part fit the rider (saddles and handlebars). Regardless, selection of a part in no way implies it has a qualitative advantage over the others; every part in this book is well designed, well crafted, and worth your consideration.

Although every item in this book is a quality piece, not every quality item is here. Why not? In some cases, it's a matter of sheer volume. There's no reason to catalog the thousands of stems and handlebars and seatposts available. In other cases, it's because the manufacturer was particularly difficult to deal with. Campagnolo, for instance, set conditions that were simply too demanding for me to meet; hence, no Campy in this book. (At least not under its own name: the Sachs components are actually made by Campagnolo and dressed up with the Sachs logos.)

If you're ordering your parts by mail, confirm that what you want is in stock and ready to ship. Get them to commit to a ship date. Try to get a date by which you can expect your order. If you're ordering through a shop, have it take the same steps with its supplier.

Strict laws govern what mail-order companies can do about back orders and delivery dates. Generally, they have to have the product to you within 30 days. If they don't, they have to offer you a chance to cancel or a specific date by which you'll receive your items. Their offer and your response must be in writing.

The best way to avoid the backorder blues is to buy what's in stock, either at your dealer's or at the catalog retailers. Some catalog houses are better than others. In years of ordering from Excel Sports in Boulder, Colorado, I've yet to be disappointed. On the other hand, I once ordered from another well-known catalog and didn't receive the last items in the order until two months later.

Pride Goeth Before the Fall There's an immense amount of pride in riding a bike you've built. But that pride quickly becomes shame if you ruin something through your incompetence.

No matter how good you tell your friends you are at wrenching, now's the time to be brutally honest with yourself. Do you really have the skill necessary to install a headset? Can you honestly say you'll build a safe set of wheels?

Two big risks emerge when you tackle something you're not qualified to do. First, you may permanently damage an expensive component. This is especially easy to do when installing a headset. Do it wrong, and your frame is trash. Bottom brackets are next on the list of must-be-done-right parts.

Second, you may jeopardize your safety. Unlike automobiles, which abound with fluff and superfluous stuff, virtually every part of a bicycle is a critical component. If your brakes fail or your handlebars come loose because you didn't install them properly, you're in for a trip to the emergency room.

If you're at all uncomfortable about something you're doing, have someone else do it. At the very least, have your work checked by a professional. If you bought your parts from a shop, they should be glad to help you out. If you've ordered elsewhere, it would be reasonable to pay the shop's regular hourly fee to have someone look over your efforts.

Some shops, either because of greed or fears of liability issues, won't inspect work done by others. They'll only help if they can do that entire assembly, whether it's building just the wheels or the entire bike. In that case, find another shop. Or find someone whose mechanical expertise you trust.

In any event, remember that the responsibility for the quality and safety of your final product ultimately rests on your shoulders. Follow the manufacturer's instructions. Study closely the steps in this book. Have someone else inspect your work or even do some of the work for you. Take whatever steps are necessary to ensure your safety and protect the value of your investment.

Record Keeping

Keep a build journal. In it, list every part you buy. Include the manufacturer's name, the model name or number, size, color, special features, tools and parts needed for maintenance and repair, cost, and any other information that seems important.

Keep all your receipts in case you ever need to make an insurance claim. A videotape of the bike, with you narrating as you point out parts, will help too. Most police departments and insurance companies have trouble believing how much a quality bike can be worth. You'll need your records to prove your loss wasn't a $129 department store bike.

Grab a Wrench

You know what you want your perfect bike to do. You've settled on a budget. You've sourced all the parts. You know what you're willing to do yourself and what you'll turn over to someone else. Now you're ready for the next step. Let's build a bike.

Chapter 3

The Frame

The big debate in bikes for several years has centered around suspension: how much and what kind. Whether you're riding on the road or off, you should weigh the pros and cons of rigid versus front suspension versus full suspension.

Decisions, Decisions Rigid bikes offer the greatest precision, lowest weight, and least complexity. They're ideal for technical riding off-road and for road riding where pavement surfaces are good.

Front suspension dramatically improves comfort, an improvement that ascends exponentially as the ride length increases. Weight and complexity penalties are minimal.

Given that front suspension is independent of frame elements, how can it affect frame choice? Frames designed for front suspension have slightly different geometry than rigid bikes; for optimum performance, it's best to know in advance if you'll be using suspension.

Full-suspension bikes are heavier and far more complex than other types. At first, they were perfect for short, intense downhill races and little else. Designers have overcome some of the early problems, and full-suspension rigs are often seen on cross-country rides.

Despite the advances, full-suspension bikes can have weak points. Most of these center around the pivot. Where it's placed and the basic design play a big role in determining how the bike performs and how durable the pivot will be.

Rear pivots are subject to stress, not only from trail shock, but also from the rider's pedaling input and body english. These stresses aren't in the plane the pivot is designed to accommodate. The result can be premature wear and sloppy handling.

Placement of the pivot makes a huge difference in pedaling efficiency. A pivot that works when the rider is using the big chainring may not work when using the small ring, or it may work when the rider is seated but not when he's standing.

I once rode a bike from a leading manufacturer for which 30 to 40 degrees of each pedal stroke was absorbed by the rear suspension; that model wound up on my short list of Bikes I Hate.

If you're considering full suspension, scrutinize the design closely. Is it strong? Is it rebuildable? If at all possible, get a test ride. Don't even consider a design that feels noodly or that sucks up pedaling power. No amount of comfort is worth that trade-off.

Why even consider full suspension? In a word, comfort. Full suspension offers the cushiest ride around, which means you ride longer and stay fresher. Whether the extra weight and complexity are worth it depend on where you ride, how you ride, and the personality of the frame you choose.

Sometimes the best suspension doesn't come from the frame or fork. SoftRide offers a full line of frames, stems, and retrofit kits that suspend the rider, not the bike. Travel is limited, and damping can be a problem, but for many applications, their products are the ideal solution. They're lightweight and simple, and require little or no

Photo 3-1

Use a long cloth measuring tape, commonly called a quilter's tape, to check alignment. You can find these tapes, which are typically 120 in. long, at most cloth and sewing supply centers.

Put one end of the tape on the right rear dropout. Bring the tape around the head tube, and back to the left rear dropout. Check the measurement, then divide that figure in half. The quotient should be the number where the tape lies at the middle of the head tube.

Use the same procedure to check other dimensions. Measure from the rear dropouts up and over the seat cluster. Also measure from the bottom bracket shell up and over the seat cluster.

Checking alignment this way is less than exact, but it will uncover problems not visible to the naked eye.

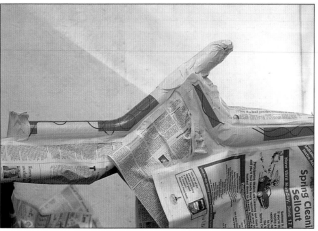

Photo 3-2

If you're going to paint your frame, now's the time to do it. First, a word of caution. Read and follow all manufacturer's instructions. The fumes from all paint products can be harmful — some more than others. Use at least a mask; a ventilator would be better. Work where there's plenty of ventilation.

Begin by masking off all areas you don't want painted. Be sure to cover everything; overspray can float a long way before slipping through a small gap in masking. Note: the blue you see is highly flexible masking tape from 3M. The areas under the tape will remain orange.

Photo 3-3

Next, prep the area to be painted by lightly sanding it with wet 600 grit sandpaper. Be sure to get all the way to the edges. The goal is to knock the shine off the factory finish so the new paint can adhere.

Clean the surface with a body shop cleaner, such as 3M's adhesive cleaner or Acry-Sol.

Apply several coats of primer according to the manufacturer's instructions.

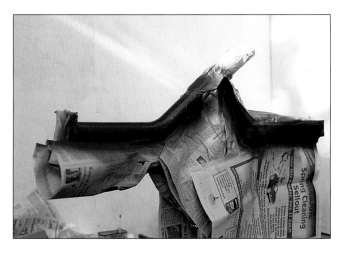

Photo 3-4

Apply several color coats. Allow adequate drying time between them. Once the color coats are dry, apply any decals, then finish with several clear coats.

After the paint has had sufficient drying time — probably at least 48 hours — carefully remove the masking. If the paint doesn't crinkle up and crack as you pull the masking tape, it hasn't fully cured yet. Let it set up another 12 hours and try again.

Check the manufacturer's suggestions regarding wet sanding and waxing the finish.

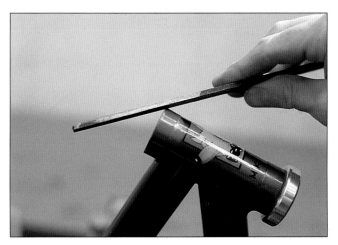

Photo 3-5

Remove the paint from the face of the head tube with a fine file. Paint left in place may crack and fall off when the headset is installed. Use the same procedure for bottom bracket shells, if required. (Cartridge-type bottom brackets, which don't make contact with the shell face, don't need this step.)

Begin with the file at a 45° angle from the top of the tube. Holding the file firmly, move it forward with light pressure against the tube. Lift the file at the end of stroke and repeat. Work your way around the tube until there's a thin (0.5 mm), continuous circle of bare metal. Don't drag the file backward over the tube; this will chip the paint and dull the file. Be careful in places where other tubes are near your work area. One small slip can put an unsightly gash in the paint.

maintenance. Most models allow the use of racks, panniers, and similar accessories, which makes them ideal for touring bikes. SoftRide models without seat tubes, however, are a challenge to secure to car racks.

In making a suspension decision, think about your needs. Arrange a test ride on any full-suspension unit you're considering. Ask yourself whether you're willing to put up with increased weight, cost, and complexity in exchange for vastly improved comfort. Talk it all over with the frame builder or supplier. Take your time; you'll live with this decision for many rides.

Pre-Building Chores

Before putting any time or money into your project, check the frame to be sure it's aligned. Builders align frames in their shop on jigs that hold extremely tight tolerances. Still, some misalignments do slip through, and some frames that are perfectly aligned at the shop get tweaked in shipping. Mass-produced frames aren't exempt from misalignments, either.

If the frame's alignment checks out OK, move on to prepping the frame itself. Anything that needs to be done to the frame should be done now; it's unlikely you'll ever have a naked frame to work with again. Some chores are necessary, some are optional. We can further divide these jobs into those you can do yourself and those it would be best to leave to others.

Let's start with necessary things that should be done by others: chase and face. *Chase* means cleaning the threads of any welding slag, paint overspray, or other debris that would prevent the proper installation of threaded parts. *Face* refers to surface finishing of the head tube and bottom bracket shell. Facing serves two functions: it removes paint and other unwanted material, and it ensures that the opposite faces are parallel.

Any professionally built frame will come chased and faced. It's unreasonable to expect an end user to perform these tasks, because the cost of the necessary tools is so high. Quality tools used to chase and face the bottom bracket cost from $300 to $1,000.

The frame builder should also chase the smaller threads in dropout eyelets and water bottle cage mounting holes to remove burrs. If it has not beem done, you can do it yourself, using a sharp tap. On the bottle cage bosses, where the screw thread does not continue into the frame tube, you'll have to use a so-called bottoming tap, which has a flat tip.

Start the tap with your fingers, trying to engage the existing threads. Once you meet resistance, go in one-half turn, then back out the tap one turn to clear any chips. Keep the tap well oiled, and proceed cautiously. Be especially careful not to chip the paint or cross-thread the hole.

The builder will face the bottom bracket shell and head tube prior to painting, which means paint will have built up around these areas. This paint should be removed in most cases. If not, the pressure of the headset or bottom bracket parts will cause the paint to fracture and chip away.

The bottom bracket shell may or may not require a final facing, depending on the type of bottom bracket you use. Those with cups that fit entirely inside the shell need no facing. Those with a traditional lockring should be faced to remove paint, a task you can do yourself if you wish.

One more step the builder should take is to ream the seat tube, which will have been distorted by the heat of welding or brazing. A seat tube that is even slightly out of round will make the installation of a seatpost nearly impossible.

For peace of mind, go through this checklist with your builder:

1. head tube faced

2. bottom bracket shell chased and faced (plus a final facing, if required for the type of bottom bracket you select)

3. eyelet and water bottle cage mounting holes chased

4. seat tube reamed

Painting There are compelling reasons not to paint your new frame. Factory paint is durable, professionally applied, and, in the case of custom builders, available in any color you choose.

If you want the builder to apply the paint, go to a body shop or automotive paint supply house. Find a color or colors you like, then give the manufacturer's name and color number to the builder. Include a sketch if it's to be a multicolor finish. House of Kolor's dazzling selection of custom colors is number one in the industry. DuPont places a close second.

Other reasons to leave the painting to someone else? Painting a bike is difficult because of all the nooks and crannies. The seat cluster, head tube, and cable guides are all challenging areas. Keeping the paint out of critical spots — such as the insides of the seat tube and bottom bracket shell — is tough. The safety precautions required when working around fumes and solvents are daunting.

Perhaps worst of all is the mere technical challenge of applying a good paint job. Producing a quality finish, free of fisheye, orange peel, sags, runs, drips, grit, and thin spots requires plenty of skill. Do you really want to learn that skill using your dream bike as the classroom?

Finally, not all frames are compatible with all paints. Bonded (glued together) frames and those made of carbon fiber or similar matrices may come apart when exposed to some paints and solvents.

If you want someone else to paint your frame, but you don't want the builder to do it, ask around at body shops to find one willing to tackle your project. Check into powder coating, which is economical and durable. Or ask your local bike shop to recommend a painter.

Photo 3-6

Once the edge is finished, start on the face. You'll again use a fine file, the wider the better. Keep the file flat against the tube and file lightly until the face of the tube is bare metal.

Use the remaining paint to gauge your progress. Using flat, even strokes, you should remove paint uniformly from the face of the tube. Stop as soon as the paint is gone; do not continue once you have bare metal. If you do, you may chip the paint or, worse, distort the tube's face.

Photo 3-7

Finish the process on the head tube by cleaning up the inside edges of the tube. Use a fine sandpaper or emery cloth. Your primary objective is to remove any burrs. Your secondary objective is to put a slight — a very slight — chamfer on the inside edge to help with installation of the pressed-in bearing races.

At the bottom bracket, the final step is to clean the threads. Remove any burrs as you did at the head tube, using a light touch to prevent damaging the threads. Then use a toothbrush or brass-bristled brush to remove any debris from the threads. Machine oil, WD-40, or a similar light lubricant may help.

Clean the tubes with a clean, soft cloth to remove any remaining metal, abrasive, paint, or other debris.

Photo 3-8

Corrosion can be a problem on all steel frame materials. Here's where an ounce of prevention.…

J. P. Weigle's Frame Saver is an antioxidant ("rustproofing") formula created especially for bikes. The instructions that come with the product are clear and inclusive. If you still have questions, J. P. himself will be glad to answer them for you.

The goal is to get fluid onto every internal surface: fork legs, main triangle, seatstays, chainstays — everything. The kit includes plastic tubes of various lengths to help reach deep into the frame.

The consistency of the product is like motor oil. It's thin enough to get into crevices, but thick enough that it doesn't all run to the bottom of the tube before it sets up.

The instructions cover everything in detail, but here are some tips to keep in mind.

1. Don't start the job unless you can do it all. This minimizes the mess and reduces the risk that an area will be overlooked for treatment.

2. Have everything you need on hand, including rags, newspaper or a drop cloth, cotton swabs, and WD-40, which is a solvent for the Frame Saver fluid.

3. The outside diameter of the plastic tubes is almost the same as the inside diameter of many frame holes. If you jam the tube into the hole and dispense product into a sealed cavity, such as a fork leg, you'll build up pressure inside. When you withdraw the tube, you release the pressure along with excess product. Two solutions: one is to drill the holes out slightly oversize. To prevent rust, make sure to repaint the holes when you're done. The second is to make the application, then cover the hole with a rag as you withdraw the tube. The rag will contain any backspray.

4. This stuff stinks, and the dripping will make a mess. Save your lungs and your floors by working outdoors.

5. To get more even coverage, wiggle the plastic tube as you dispense the product. Also, try to hit every tube from more than one point. Chainstays may be accessible from the bottom bracket shell and vent holes in the dropout ends. Seatstays may only be open at the vent holes; same with the fork legs. The tubes in the main triangle should be open on both ends; you can also squirt Frame Saver through the water bottle cage mounting holes (if you drill and tap through the frame tube).

6. Also to ensure even coverage, rotate the entire frame as you're working and after you're finished.

7. To minimize dripping, plug all holes when you're done spraying. Masking tape or rags work for bigger tubes. Snap a cotton swab in half and use the stick to block vent holes. Leave the holes covered for at least 48 hours, longer if you can stand to wait before you build. Frame Saver was still weeping from this frame a week after application.

8. Protect your floors by putting newspaper or a drop cloth under the frame while the Frame Saver cures. Some fluid will ooze out despite your best efforts to contain it. Protect yourself while you're working by wearing old clothes. Rubber gloves, if you can stand to wear them while you work, keep the product off your hands, and hence off the frame, your tools, your hair, and anything else you touch.

In view of all this, why would you want to paint your frame yourself? Creative control. Pride of accomplishment. The joy of the process.

Despite the demands, painting is fun. Just be sure to take your time, perform each step correctly and completely, observe all safety procedures, and follow all manufacturer's directions.

Complete painting instructions are beyond the scope of this book, but a general overview would include four steps:

1. Prep the frame. Sand it lightly with fine (400 to 600 grit) sandpaper. If it's bare metal, make sure the metal is sanded free of rust. If it's already painted, sand only enough to knock the shine off the paint. Clean the surface with an appropriate solvent and a tack cloth.

2. Apply a primer. The type of primer is determined by the type of paint you're using and the surface condition — painted or bare metal.

3. Apply several color coats. Make sure the paint is compatible with the surface; enamels are generally safe for all applications, whereas lacquers can cause blistering of old finishes. (Why use lacquers at all? Their wide range of colors and quick drying time make them appealing.) After the final color coat, apply any stickers or decals. Make sure they're intended for outdoor use, or the sun's ultraviolet rays will fade them quickly.

4. Apply at least one clear coat.

Custom paint is the most noticeable attribute of a bike, and is thus well worth the effort. There are only two questions: How do you want it to look, and who's going to do it?

Preservation Many builders pooh-pooh the idea of rustproofing, claiming that quality steel is slow to oxidize. Owners, however, often appreciate that the slight extra effort and minimal added weight make the process worthwhile.

J. P. Weigle's Frame Saver spray is made just for this purpose. It's inexpensive and easy to apply. Follow the manufacturer's clear, complete instructions exactly and you'll have no problems.

Final Preparations After you've prepped and painted and chased and faced, go over the entire frame and remove any tapping oil, paint overspray, masking tape residue, metal shavings, or other foreign material. Use caution so you don't scratch the paint.

The last prep step is to wax the frame. Again, it's not likely you'll have a chance to wax a naked frame later, so do it now while it's convenient. (If you painted the frame, check the paint manufacturer's recommendations to see how long you should wait before waxing and whether there are any precautions about what type of wax to use.)

That's it. Your frame's as ready as it's going to get. Next, we'll install the headset and the fork.

Chapter 4

Headset and Fork

Assuming you've selected a quality frame, one in which rigidity is not an issue, the most important factor in controlling your bike is the quality of the headset and fork. Screaming downhill at 50 mph is no time to regret scrimping on these components.

The Headset

It's easy to underestimate the importance of a quality headset. A headset is almost completely concealed. It's not subjected to high rpm. The loads placed on it seem negligible. It doesn't require frequent maintenance. It doesn't affect fit. It's neither flashy nor particularly expensive. So why agonize over selecting the proper headset?

For several reasons. First, the loads transmitted through a headset *are* significant. While you're riding, every bump and

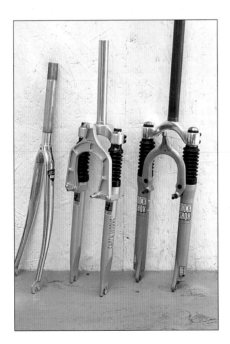

Photo 4-1

Left to right: The Kinesis road fork is made of 6061 aluminum. The blades are bonded to the crown. The steel steerer is threaded.

Kinesis forks are known for their light weight (1 lb. 3 oz. for this one), precise steering, and excellent ride quality.

The Shock Works Enforcer is typical of air-oil shocks, including the Paris-Roubaix road model seen on the SoftRide. The Enforcer has a Schrader valve atop each leg for adjusting air pres-

sure; recommended operating pressure range is 40 to 50 lbs. A small hand pump with a gauge is included.

The valves are normally covered with a plastic cap that turns to adjust damping. Fork action varies considerably between the number 1 and the number 6 settings.

At 3 lb. 14 oz., with a 1 in. threadless steerer, the Enforcer is at the heavy end of the range for this type of fork.

The Rock Shox Judy XC represents the best of urethane forks. Microcellular urethane springs pro-

vide an excellent ride with good damping; compression damping is further controlled by an adjustable oil cartridge in the left leg. Spring preload is adjustable. Six urethane springs in the right leg can be individually changed out to accommodate a wide range of rider weights and ambient temperatures.

This Judy, with a 1⅛ in. thread*less* steerer, weighed 3 lb. 12 oz.

obstruction finds its way to the headset. A 160 lb. rider traveling at 18 mph generates significant force when encountering a 1 in. pavement seam. That force is dramatically higher when riding off-road.

This impact force is multiplied by the distance from the pavement to the headset. Worst of all, when it finally arrives at the headset bearings, the force is not delivered along the load path the bearings are designed to handle, but instead is perpendicular to it.

The same leverage principle that multiplies loads also magnifies slop. A headset that's even a little loose will produce lots of scary moments as the front wheel follows road irregularities with a mind of its own.

Photo 4-2

Left to right: King Team headset in red, King Team NoThreadset in silver, Dia-Compe ThreadHead in silver, and Shimano 600 in silver. All are 1 in.

Nomenclature varies according to the source. For our purposes, we'll refer to the bearing races, which are sometimes called "cups," as the pressed-in races. There's an upper and a lower pressed-in race; they fit in either end of the head tube. The race that fits down onto the fork is the crown race.

On threaded headsets, there's also a threaded race. This is the part used to adjust the fork. Once the adjustment has been made, the threaded race is held in position by a locknut.

Photo 4-3

In the center is the "star-fangled" nut used with threadless headsets. The stem bolt threads into this nut and provides preload on the headset bearings.

To the left of the star-fangled nut is Park's installation tool. The tool ensures that the nut is installed square to the bore of the steerer, and that it is set to exactly the right depth.

To the right is the Conix device that replaces the star-fangled nut. It is removable, reusable, and does not requires a special installation tool.

Although it's true that headsets require infrequent maintenance, it's not true that they can be completely ignored. Over time, the combination of force and misadjustment leads to a condition called brinelling — the bearings hammer little indentations into the headset races. At first, the steering feels notchy rather than smooth. In extreme cases, "index steering" can result, during which the fork automatically tries to center itself.

Suddenly the lowly headset takes on new importance. The wisdom of buying a quality model that offers durable parts and easy servicing becomes clear.

In years past, durability and serviceability were the only considerations. Then Dia-Compe came along with their AheadSet threadless headset and muddied the waters. Now most manufacturers offer a threadless headset; in fact, some offer only threadless models.

The big advantage of threadless headsets is reduced weight. Paired with the right stem, a threadless headset may reduce weight by 50 percent compared to a traditional headset and stem combination. In some cases, it's also easier to maintain proper bearing adjustment with threadless headsets.

Disadvantages? First, adjusting handlebar height is difficult. Unlike traditional stems, which have virtually infinite height adjustment, threadless stems rely on stacks of washers to shim their height. The result is limited adjustability that is more difficult to accomplish than with traditional stems.

Limited adjustability makes it even more critical that you select the right components from the beginning. Even then, tweaking the fit to adapt to your body's changing flexibility as the season progresses can be a nuisance.

The other drawback to the stack-of-washers approach is that you gain back some of the weight you shed by going to a threadless headset in the first place. And depending on the style of the washers, the appearance can be rather "home-spun."

The second drawback to threadless headsets is that the star-fangled nut can be a problem. It must be installed to exactly the right depth in the fork. Once installed, it's all but impossible to remove. (Fortunately, it's unlikely you'd ever need to do so.) Conix solved this problem with an inexpensive, good-looking aftermarket replacement part.

Evaluate the weight, serviceability, and height adjustment issues for yourself to determine whether a traditional or threadless headset is right for your bike. Whatever style you choose, go with a quality product, such as those made by King, Dia-Compe, or Shimano.

The fundamental decision in selecting a headset involves size. *Sutherland's* lists more than a half-dozen different head tube diameters to fit a corresponding variety of headsets. Fortunately, the industry has settled on two common sizes for most quality bikes: 1 in. and 1⅛ in.

The other dimension to consider is stack height. This is basically the combined measurement of how much the headset protrudes above and below the head tube with all its parts in place. When building a new bike, stack height isn't important because the fork's steerer tube will be cut to length.

When replacing a worn-out headset, however, stack height becomes critical. It's best to replace the headset with an identical component, which means you should choose a model now that will be available and will make you happy for as long as you own your bike.

Campagnolo headsets have some peculiarities. If you choose to use a Campy headset, talk to your builder to make sure your frame will accommodate it.

The Road Bike Fork

If you're building anything but a mountain bike, chances are your frame came with a fork. That's both good and bad. Good because you probably saved money on a competent fork. Bad because it may not be the right fork for you.

How do forks vary? First, in ride characteristics. A strong, 230 lb. person riding aggressively needs something very different from a gentle, 120 lb. rider. Compliance is another issue; what one person finds comfortable another considers too imprecise.

Second, forks vary in aesthetics. Do you prefer the modernistic appearance of a unicrown design, where the fork blades curve and meet at the top? Or would you rather have the classic elegance of a Henry James crown, for which the blades are fillet brazed into place?

Third, forks vary in function. Do you need dropout eyelets for a fender and rack? What about mid-fork attachment points for a lowrider-type rack?

Chances are good that the fork supplied with your frame will be at least adequate for your needs. If you decide later that it's not, replacing a fork is relatively easy, although not cheap.

The best idea is to discuss your needs with the builder. Some things, such as the number and placement of eyelets, will be up to you. Some, such as the type of crown and blade material, will be a joint decision. Other things, such as the amount of rake, are better left entirely to the builder.

The Evolution of Suspension Forks

For years, a mountain bike fork was just a road fork on steroids: same basic design, but beefier. The suspension fork boom of the late 1980s changed all that.

Experimentation and available technology pushed suspension forks through hundreds of design iterations in just a few years. From this, some truths emerged.

Photo 4-4 (right)

The Park bearing press is the correct tool for installing headset pressed-in races. It has adapters to fit various sizes of bearings. The force is applied to the perimeter of the race, not the bearing surface, to prevent damage. Its large, flat driving surfaces help hold the races square against

the head tube. The beefy handles provide plenty of leverage.

The end opposite the handles is held in place with a spring release that fits into a series of notches on the post. The tool works with the handle at either end of the head tube.

Park's instructions are complete, but here are some tips:

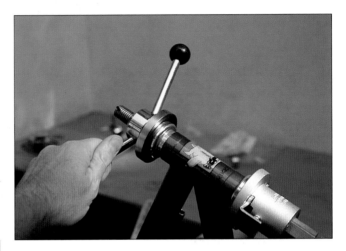

1. Make sure the head tube has been properly prepared (see Chapter 3).

2. Apply a coat of antiseize compound inside the head tube to ease installation and facilitate future replacement.

3. Make sure the races enter the head tube squarely. The tool makes it difficult — but not impossible — to cram the races in at an angle, which can ruin the frame.

4. Be careful installing and withdrawing the tool. Banging a race with the tool shaft could damage a bearing surface.

5. When the races are seated against the head tube — STOP. The Park press is a heavy-duty tool that can develop enough pressure to distort the races.

Photo 4-5 (bottom left)

If you choose not to buy the Park press and still want to install the headset yourself, a length of threaded rod with some fender washers will do the trick. The big problem is that without the press, it's very difficult to hold the race square to the head tube. You'll have to be patient, because the races *must* be driven straight.

Air-oil forks, which use compressed gas for springing and oil for damping, offer outstanding ride and tuneability. Unlike other materials, air has a spring rate that rises exponentially with travel, which means that an air fork is compliant on small bumps yet resists bottoming on big bumps.

These forks also offer superior damping, which is the ability to control spring action. By using different viscosities of oil, damping can be adjusted to meet the needs of a wide range of riders. Best of

Photo 4-6

Here's what you'll need to install the fork crown race (left to right): a wooden block to support the fork by the crown, a section of pipe to drive the race, the fork, masking tape, and a hammer. Not shown: antiseize compound and the crown race.

The block supports the fork by the crown to keep the dropout tips from being damaged. It's also easier to keep the fork upright if it's supported this way.

The pipe must have the correct inside diameter to drive the crown race by the race's inside lip. The pipe must *not* strike the bearing surface of the race.

Wrap the steerer tube threads in masking tape to prevent damage to them. You can get at least two layers over the threads and still slip the pipe easily over the tape.

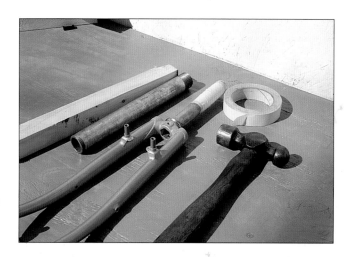

Photo 4-7

With the fork supported by the crown with a wooden block, carefully drive the crown race. Tap the pipe, rotate it a quarter turn, tap it again. After the fourth tap, check the race to see that it's being driven squarely. If not, try another round with the pipe. If necessary, remove the pipe and use a punch to drive down the high side of the race.

Again, be careful not to damage the bearing surface. And don't allow the race to get badly misaligned. If the difference in distance between any two points of the race and the crown is more than 0.5 mm, stop and square up the race before attempting to drive it any farther.

all, forks with external adjusting knobs offer trailside damping adjustments. A twist of the knob changes the size of the orifice through which the oil is passed inside the fork, making damping faster or slower.

The most sophisticated motorcycle and automotive suspensions use air-oil components. The "air" is often nitrogen, and the oil is kept separate from the gas to prevent foaming.

Air-oil shocks aren't perfect, however. Air doesn't like to be under pressure, and keeping it inside the fork requires complicated seals. These seals must fit tightly against the fork sliders (lower legs), which causes static friction, or "stiction." This makes the fork unresponsive to small bumps, because it takes a large impact to overcome the stiction. The seals are also prone to failure. This usually happens during a ride, which means returning with the fork completely collapsed, or "sacked."

Some manufacturers sought to improve on air-oil shocks by replacing the air with metal springs. This solved the seal problem, but weight went up significantly. Progressivity was lost too, as even the best progressive-wound coil springs can't mimic the spring rate of air under compression.

Elastomer Forks
Elastomer forks, which use compressible foam for both spring and damping, offer many advantages. They're light, simple, and easy to service. They can be tuned by using elastomers of different stiffness. In models with stacks of separate elastomers (as compared to those with a single, long elastomer), tuneability is quite good.

Drawbacks? Elastomer performance varies with temperature; a fork that is compliant in summer is nearly rigid in winter. Also, because the elastomers are solely responsible for spring rate, compression damping, and rebound damping, it's difficult to find exactly the right ones for best all-around performance.

Two design changes dramatically improved elastomer forks. The first was the use of improved elastomers made of microcellular urethane (MCU). These MCU elastomers offered better damping, and were more resistant to changes in performance due to temperature. The second was the use of a separate oil cartridge to further improve damping.

There are other problems associated with suspension forks, and other solutions to address them. The first problem is independent leg movement.

Depending on a number of conditions, forces transmitted into the fork are rarely equally applied to both legs, nor are they in direct line with the intended fork leg movement. This creates side stress, or thrust, that can cause the upper and lower fork legs to twist, bend, and bind where they overlap.

To cure this, manufacturers took several steps. One was to increase the size of the front hub, axle, and skewer. Another was to improve the fork seals. Another was to increase the overlap between the stanchions and slider tubes. All these helped ensure that the legs would move in unison.

Another problem was the effect of braking on the upper legs. Cantilever brakes exert force inward on the rim. Newton tells us there's an equal and opposite outward force where the brakes attach to the fork legs. This tends to bow the legs outward, reducing fork performance.

The solution to brake-induced flex was to put a better support arch between the cantilever bosses. Fork manufacturers offer good ones; the best models are still found in the aftermarket. These arches not only help under braking; they also make the fork stiffer under all conditions.

Not everyone trod the same path when trying to overcome the problems of suspension forks. Cannondale, for example, put the suspension in the head tube. Girvin introduced a parallelogram mechanism that eliminated sliders. Most of these unique designs were effective. But as traditional suspension forks began offering longer travel, the other designs often couldn't keep up.

Suspension forks have evolved so that now most of them offer excellent performance and reliability. Air-oil still affords the best ride and tuneability, but the best elastomer forks are approaching that level of performance. And although air-oil seals are infinitely better than earlier generations, elastomer forks still side-step this issue.

Selecting Forks How do you select the right fork? A quality fork from a leading manufacturer will provide performance that is at least very good, if not outstanding, so look beyond the immediate. Does the fork offer a full range of adjustability? Is it adjustable on the trail, or does adjustment require disassembly? Is the fork easily rebuildable? How often is service required? Even 100-hour service intervals are too frequent; it doesn't take many rides to rack up 100 hours.

Are aftermarket parts, such as brake bridges, available? Does the fork accommodate the type of brakes you want to use?

Do some additional research. Have there been any recalls of the fork you're considering? Any reports of failure? One leading

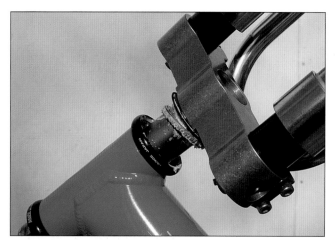

Photo 4-8

Cartridge bearings need no preparation prior to installation. Caged or loose bearings should be greased before they're installed. If they came greased, clean off the factory grease and regrease with a bicycle-specific product.

Caged bearings must be oriented properly. Notice that on one edge, there's a continuous metal band. On the other, the ball bearings themselves peek above the cage. The edge with the continuous band should face away from the head tube. In other words, that band should face toward the crown race on the bottom and toward the lockring on the top.

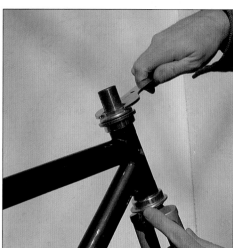

Photo 4-9

Install the fork and tighten the threaded race. We'll fine-tune the adjustment later. For now it need only be close, not perfect. The fork should have no noticeable play, yet should turn freely.

Photo 4-10

Install the locknut, any washers, brake cable hanger, spacers, and other items. Measure the remaining gap between the last part and the threaded race. This measurement is critical, so take your time and get it right. Take the measurement several times from different sides. And use the best measuring tool you have. Calipers are good. I'm using a machinist's rule, which is graduated in 64ths of an inch.

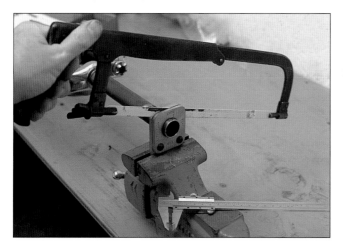

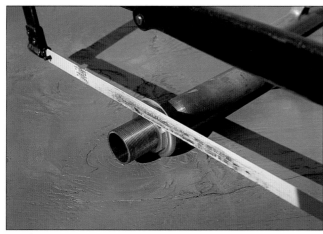

Photo 4-11

If you'll be using a spacer between the locknut and the threaded race, subtract its height from the measurement you got in photo 4-10.

Measure the steerer tube. Again, this measurement is critical; take your time and measure repeatedly to make sure you get it right.

The Park saw guide tools for cutting steerer tubes come in three sizes for threaded types, and one universal model for threadless. They hold the steerer securely. A tab on the tool mounts in a vise to keep everything in place while you cut. The guides ensure a square cut.

It's hard to tell how far down the steerer the guide needs to be. Start the cut before putting the steerer into the guide so you'll have a reference point.

With the threaded type, screw the tool onto the steerer so that the threaded end of the tool faces the fork crown. Then, when the tool is removed, the threaded part will clean up the steerer threads.

Use a fine-tooth blade: 22 or 24 teeth per inch.

The threads will probably need to be dressed with a very fine file, such as a jeweler's file, after you've made the cut and removed the tool. Look closely to see which threads, if any, have been damaged.

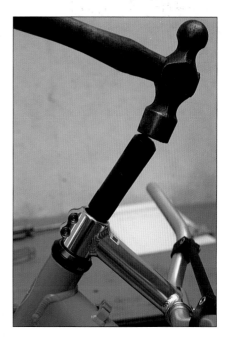

Pay special attention to where the threads start at the end of the steerer.

Also clean up the inside of the steerer. Remove any burrs with a file, emery cloth, or fine sandpaper.

Photo 4-12 (center)

If you choose not to use Park's saw guides, you can use the locknut or the threaded race as a guide. It will be difficult to hold the blade square because it will want to follow the threads. If the blade pulls into the nut or race, it can damage it. So cut slowly and watch your progress closely.

Photo 4-13

Whereas a threaded headset is adjusted by the threaded race, a threadless model relies on a bolt and the star-fangled nut or similar part to increase or decrease pressure on the bearings.

(continued on page 48)

(continued from page 47)

With the star-fangled nut in place, the stem is installed. The bolt from the stem into the star-fangled nut is used to adjust the headset. Follow the manufacturer's directions, taking care especially not to over-tighten this bolt.

Installing the star-fangled nut requires attention to two details. First, the nut must be driven square to the steerer tube. Second, it must be driven to exactly the right depth. Again, Park makes a series of tools for this job.

manufacturer's fork was prone to breakage about 6 in. above the dropouts. Aftermarket manufacturers had to move the support arm for their disk brakes much farther up the fork. Otherwise, the stresses from braking would snap the fork.

Talk to the fork manufacturer or a knowledgeable person at a bike shop, to see what brakes and hubs they recommend for use with the fork you're considering.

Once you've selected a model, be sure to follow the instructions for installation and servicing. If your fork doesn't come with boots, consider adding them. Keeping grit off the sliders will prolong the life of the seals.

The only widely available road bike suspension fork is the Paris-Roubaix model from Rock Shox. It is an air-oil style. The design helps keep the weight down, but it's still about twice as heavy as a quality rigid aluminum road fork.

The Paris-Roubaix is an ideal application for air-oil technology. Because a road fork is subjected to less punishment than a mountain bike fork, the Paris-Roubaix doesn't suffer from seal failure, stiction, and independent leg movement the way an air-oil mountain bike fork may.

Tools and Installation

Be careful when installing a headset. If it's misaligned, you could ruin your frame. Before installing the headset, consider whether this is something better left to a shop.

If you do decide to proceed, the best option is to use the tools specifically designed for the job. The Park bearing press is a quality tool that will keep the parts properly aligned during installation, minimizing the risk of frame damage.

If you can't borrow a Park press, and if you don't want to buy your own, you can use a length of threaded rod with fender washers instead. This is *not* a recommended procedure though, because holding the parts in alignment is very difficult. If you try this, work slowly, and watch the races to be sure they remain square to the head tube.

Whatever method you use, be sure the driving force during installation is applied to the outer edges of the races. Applying force to the bearing surfaces can damage them.

Some amateur mechanics advocate installing the headset using the fork as a press. They assemble the parts, including the fork, then tighten the top nut. Bad idea. This puts the force directly on the bearing surfaces. It may also strip the threads on the steerer.

Drive the fork crown race into place with a suitable piece of pipe. Cover the steerer threads with masking tape to prevent damage to them. Make sure the pipe is driving against the inside lip of the race, not the bearing surface.

Use antiseize compound between the crown race and the fork, and between the pressed-in races and the head tube. No matter how good this headset is, some day you'll want to replace it. Without antiseize, that may be impossible.

Clean the bearings before installing them, then apply grease. A bicycle-specific grease is preferred, but any good waterproof grease will do.

The headset is properly adjusted when all the play is out of it. Grab the lower part of the fork and try to rock it back and forth. If there's any play, the headset is too loose. Also rotate the fork from side to side. If there's any resistance, or if you feel a rumbling, the headset is too tight.

Work slowly. When adjusting the headset, an eighth of a turn may be all there is between too loose and too tight. Try to rock and rotate the fork with the headset slightly loose and slightly tight. Feel the difference? The headset is correct when it's just tight enough that all play has been removed.

Threadless headsets are adjusted with the stem in place. The stem bolt engages the star-fangled nut. Be careful. It's easy to tighten the bolt too much. This puts excessive preload on the bearings and will lead to their premature failure. Checking the adjustment is done the same way as for traditional headsets.

Taking Shape With the fork installed, your project is beginning to look like a bicycle. Still, something's lacking. Wheels. They're next on our agenda.

Photo 4-14

Regardless of headset type, the goal of adjustment is the same: remove all play from the fork without inhibiting its free rotation.

Check for play by holding the frame with one hand and the fork with the other. Try to rock the fork back and forth. If you feel any looseness, tighten the threaded race on a threaded headset or the stem bolt on a threadless type.

Once all play is eliminated, rotate the fork to be sure the headset isn't too tight. If you feel any resistance or any rumbling, loosen the appropriate part.

The easiest way to get the proper adjustment is to work backward from excessive play to zero play, rather than from too-tight to not-too-tight. As you approach the correct adjustment, turning the race or bolt even a few degrees will make a noticeable difference.

Once you have the adjustment correct, tighten the locknut on a threaded headset. (With a threadless style, you're done once the adjustment is finished.) Hold the threaded race with a headset wrench while tightening the locknut. Check the fork again to be sure it's still properly adjusted. If not, you may be able to correct the problem by slightly turning both the threaded race and the locknut simultaneously in a counterclockwise direction.

Chapter 5

The Wheels

For many years, wheels were behind the development curve. While technology brought us new frame materials, lightweight components, and index shifting, wheels were still just metal hoops connected to simple hubs by wire spokes.

Wheels Old and New In fact, most wheels are built today as they were a hundred years ago. Why? Because the traditional style of wheel building produces

Photo 5-1

Cronometro's road wheels — the mountain versions are on the Crosstrac — have 16, 18, or 20 spokes in the front and 28 in the rear.

The spokes are straight-pull, which makes them much stronger. Nipples are moved from the rim to the hub; lightweight hubs are used. The result is a wheel that's noticeably easier to accelerate, is less turbulent than other spoked wheels, is less susceptible to crosswinds than other aero wheels, and suffers no loss of reliability.

Photo 5-2

Spinergy's Rev-X Roks mountain bike wheels — the road versions are on the SoftRide — are popular aero wheels.

The minimal penalties in weight and slightly increased sensitivity to crosswinds compared to traditional spoked wheels are more than made up for by superior aerodynamics. Best of all, their ride is nearly indistinguishable from traditional spoked wheels.

an excellent product. Wire wheels are light, strong, easy to maintain, and affordable.

Then why the recent push for exotic wheels? Because wire wheels, despite their strengths, have a few problems as well.

Spinergy and other composite wheel manufacturers sought to minimize one of those problems: turbulence. Wire wheels churn the air as they turn, creating considerable turbulence and drag. This drag increases exponentially with speed.

Composite wheels replace many wire spokes with a few flat ones. Reducing the number of spokes reduces drag. But the real gain comes in spoke design. The composite spokes are flat in cross section, which encourages laminar air flow.

Composite wheels have their own drawbacks. They're heavier than wire spoke wheels. Handling can suffer in a crosswind. There's no way to service them; if a spoke gets damaged, the entire wheel must be replaced. Early models had excessive flex, which resulted in poor handling. Composites are notch-sensitive, which means a scratch on the surface can result in failure. And composite wheels are expensive. Manufacturers continue to address these concerns, and their wheels are improving rapidly.

Cronometro took a different approach to solving the problems associated with traditional wire wheels. They kept the wire spokes, but used fewer of them. This reduced weight and drag. Ordinarily, it would also increase failure, but Cronometro changed other design parameters, too.

The weak point with traditional spokes is the bend where the spoke exits the hub. Cronometro eliminated this bend by using special hubs that permit straight-pull spokes.

Fewer spokes mean less drag. Cronometro further improved performance by moving the spoke nipples from the rim to the hub. This may seem like an insignificant change, but it's hard to accelerate rotating mass, and moving that mass closer to the center of the wheel results in wheels with less inertia, so they respond faster to the rider's input.

Cronometro wheels are light, strong, and fast. The bad news: they're also expensive.

For builders on a budget, it's tough to beat a set of traditional spoked wheels. The decision then becomes whether to build them yourself or buy them already built up. The charge for building a wheel is reasonable; unless you're a very fast wheel builder, you're only paying yourself a few dollars an hour to do the job. Add in the cost of the tools you'll need, and there is no economic justification for building your own wheels. On the other hand, purchasing tools now means you'll have them on hand the next time you need them.

Beyond economics, there's a mystical allure to building wheels. Along with frame construction and painting, wheel building is the one other process in assembling a bike that's referred to as an art. In truth, it requires no magic — just plenty of patience.

The Numbers You Need In building wheels, there are several dimensions that must be known. They're used to determine spoke length. Most of these come from the manufacturers, although you can measure them yourself. In most cases, you won't need to know the actual numbers, because spokes can be ordered simply by matching rims and hubs on a chart or with software.

Still, it's good to know what all these figures mean. It helps you talk intelligently to manufacturers and bike shop people. And the day may come when you want to order spokes for an obscure or discontinued hub or rim. If the dimensions aren't on a chart somewhere, you'll have to come up with them on your own.

Write all the dimensions for the wheels you're building in your build journal.

The first number is the hub's over-locknut dimension. This is the distance from the face of the left locknut to the face of the right locknut; it corresponds to the space between the dropouts. For front hubs, this distance is usually 100 mm. For rear hubs, common sizes are 130 and 135 mm, with some older 126 mm hubs still around.

It's important to use a hub that is the right size for your frame. Stretching or compressing the rear triangle even 5 mm can cause damage (although it's unlikely). Never use the quick-release skewer to retain a 130 mm hub in 135 mm dropouts.

The next number refers to the pattern you'll use. Three-cross is the most common. It provides a comfortable ride, precise handling, and good durability. The name refers to the number of other spokes each spoke crosses.

Other patterns exist, including radial. In radial lacing, spokes run directly from the hub to the rim without crossing any other spokes. The pattern makes for a light, rigid wheel. But because road shock is transmitted directly along the spoke, durability of radially laced wheels is not good. In fact, most hub manufacturers' warranties exclude radial-laced wheels. Radial lacing also requires much more precise measuring of other dimensions to ensure proper spoke length.

Photo 5-4 (center right)

Technology has made inroads into road tires. The Vittoria Tecno Twin Tread tires on the Mikkelsen bike are one example. But technology is rampant in mountain bike tires, where manufacturers can play with not only compound and casing specifications but lug design and pattern as well.

(Top to bottom) Wilderness Trail Bikes offers their VelociRaptor for rear or front applications. Ritchey's Alphabite is for the front, the Omegabite for the rear. All are excellent tires, although not equally at home in varying conditions. To determine what tire is best for where you ride, ask around. Try different tires whenever you get the chance. Performance varies widely, and a test ride is often the only way to know for sure how a tire will match up with your style and abilities and the conditions in which you ride.

Photo 5-3 (top left)

Here's a traditional wheel, albeit a very nice one. Components are a Sun CR18 rim, Ringle hub, Kore quick release, DT Swiss stainless steel 14-gauge spokes, and a Ritchey Alphabite tire. Although the performance isn't quite equal to the best aero wheels, neither is the cost. You could build two of these wheels for the cost of two aero wheels and have enough left over to pay for most of your frame.

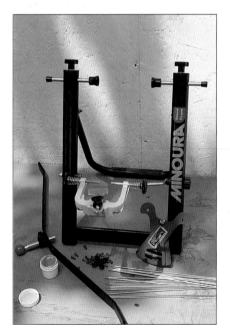

Photo 5-5 (bottom left)

Here's what you need to build a wheel. Clockwise from the lower left are Wheelsmith Spoke Prep, dishing tool and truing stand from Minoura, Wheelsmith spoke tensiometer, spokes, and in the center, nipples.

The Minoura tools are homeowner quality and generally work quite well. The truing stand isn't as fast to use as a professional model, nor does it hold every hub as securely. But then it doesn't have the pro model's price, either.

The spokes are straight 14-gauge DT Swiss stainless, and the nipples are from Spline Drive. They're anodized alloy.

The greatest feature is the spline drive: instead of four flat driving surfaces, Spline Drive nipples have six. The advantage: they're much less likely to round off, because the force is distributed to 50 percent more area. The disadvantage: they require a special tool. Spline Drive has both shop and seat-pack styles available. But if you lose yours or leave it at home, it's unlikely any other rider you encounter will have a spoke wrench to fit.

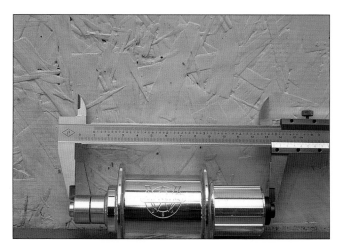

Photo 5-6

Mountain Bike Hubs
From top left: White Industries' Tracker front hub is completely user serviceable, using only a 2 mm Allen wrench, included with the hub.

The Aft-Tracker cassette hub from White Industries is also user serviceable. It has four bearings and three pawls. Spacers provided with the hub allow it to fit 130 or 135 mm dropout spacing and accept either 7- or 8-speed Shimano cassettes.

In front of those two hubs is the Wilderness Trail Bikes New Paradigm hub. Its two bearings are spaced as far apart as possible to give best support, and they are adjustable to compensate for wear. The left side has a Grease Guard grease injection port. The literature accompanying the hub gives a compelling argument (and instructions) for building wheels with a 7-speed cog set to reduce dish and improve wheel strength.

Next are the Shimano XT Parallax hubs. No "oh-wow" features on these. They're acceptably light, have a straightforward design, and come with quick releases. Perfectly competent hubs for most applications, from the industry leader.

In front are Ringlé hubs. The Superdupereight rear includes a spacer to adapt to 7-speed cog sets. It also has full service instructions, including information on lubricating the pawls. The Superduperbubba front has D-shaped axle ends to better engage the fork's dropout slots and thereby reduce fork flex. It also has a large, 25.4 mm clamping surface to further improve rigidity. The large surface area precludes use with some popular forks.

Photo 5-7

Road Hubs: The American Classic Speed Hub front hub has a 16 mm alloy axle and a 7075-T6 shell. It's available in 12- through 36-hole drilling. The rear Speed Hub (not shown) is threaded for a freewheel, one of the few hubs still available that will accommodate a freewheel. American Classic also makes track hubs and a freehub for use with cassettes.

In the center are Shimano 105 hubs, and to the right of them are their 600 Ultegra models. Both styles are 8-speed compatible and include quick releases. They're easy to service, reasonably light, and not unattractive.

Photo 5-8

The over-locknut dimension is easy to get. It will most likely be either 130 mm or 135 mm in the rear. This White Industries hub is 135 mm.

The next number: hub flange diameter. This is the center-to-center distance between two opposite spoke holes in the flange. *Sutherland's* lists ten categories of flange diameters — from 31 mm to 102.5 mm — each of which represents a range. For example, the 58 mm category includes sizes from 53 to 60 mm.

The next measurement is hub center to flange center. As the name implies, this is the distance from the center of the hub to the center of the flange. On front hubs, the left and right measurements are the same. On rear hubs, the right (drive) side distance is less than the left.

The obvious rim dimension is diameter. This can be measured using special rods. The rods are inserted through opposite spoke holes. Where they overlap in the center of the rim, one rod has a scale and the other has an index mark. The index mark points to the rim diameter on the scale.

Instead of actual diameter, some charts use a "rim correction factor." This number is subtracted from a value computed from the other dimensions. The final result is the spoke length.

The Sum of Its Parts Whether you build your own wheels or buy them built, think first about the individual parts.

Rims

The first decision in selecting a rim is the number of holes. Recently, 32-hole rims have become the standard for both road and mountain bikes. Touring bikes should have 36-hole rims; tandems may have up to 48 holes. (Hole count is always in multiples of four.)

Rim style is partly controlled by tire choice. The first choice is between clincher and sew-up. Because modern clincher tires are so close in performance to sew-ups, few people submit to the frustration of using sew-ups any more. Rim selection is better with clincher styles, too.

Another aspect of tire choice that affects rim selection is width. Standard road tire widths run from 19 mm to 23 or 25 mm. Touring and city bike tires run from 25 mm up to 38 mm. Heavier riders, and those who frequently ride poorly paved streets, need tires at the wider end of this range. Mountain bike tires are measured in inches, with widths of 1.75 to 2.25 in. being common. Consider the width of tire you'll use, then make sure the rim you select is suitable for that tire.

Manufacturing a good rim is a balancing act. On one side, you have every feature that contributes to a strong rim, such as thick side walls, a box cross section, and eyelets to prevent cracking around the spoke holes. On the other side, there is weight. Big, aggressive riders must accept either a weight penalty for strong rims or the likely prospect of wheel failure.

Besides width and weight, a few other features warrant consideration. Most manufacturers offer some type of coating, usually ceramic, on the sidewalls to improve braking. Modern brakes, whether cantilever or caliper, stop so well in dry weather that the value of such coatings is questionable. But in some environments, notably wet conditions, the coatings can increase braking efficiency dramatically.

One other thing to consider is color. Anodized center sections come not only in solid colors but also in an array of multicolors and patterns. Choose whatever you like — as long as the sides are not anodized (because it negatively effects braking).

Hubs

Hubs also come anodized. What features do you look for besides finish?

Hubs used with suspension forks should have oversized axles to help maintain alignment and steering precision. The mating surface between the hub and dropout is larger, and the axle itself has a larger diameter to better resist flexing.

At one time, the way to build a rigid wheel was to use a hub with a high flange. Although the days of absurdly high hub flanges are gone, flange style still matters. Some manufacturers angle the flanges in slightly, to reduce stress on spokes. This becomes more important with small rim diameters and high flanges, a combination found on some mountain bike wheels.

Hub bearings are subjected to high loads. They're also subjected to road grit and water. Sealed cartridge bearings work well in this environment, although traditional caged or loose bearings are fine as long as the hub seals are in good shape. Remember that all hub bearings, whether cartridge, caged, or loose, will require attention at some point. Make sure the hub you select is serviceable. Avoid hubs for which bearing replacement is difficult or requires special tools.

Perhaps the most important feature of a rear hub is one you can't see without taking the hub apart. Inside are tiny parts, called

Photo 5-9

Notice how the center line of the hub is not equidistant from the center lines of the flanges. The outermost lines are the over-locknut lines; they are 135 mm apart. The middle line is the center line of the hub, and it is of course equidistant from the over-locknut lines (67.5 mm). But the hub's center line is only 19.5 mm from the right flange, whereas it is 34.0 mm from the left flange.

Likewise, the flanges aren't equidistant from the locknuts. The right flange is 48.0 mm from the right locknut; the left flange is 33.5 mm from the left locknut.

If your hub or rim isn't on the charts, you'll need to know all these dimensions before you can order spokes. The dimensions should be given in the literature that came with the hub, or you may have to call the manufacturer. Worst case: measure the dimensions yourself.

Photo 5-10

Flange diameter is the other dimension you'll need when ordering spokes. Measure directly across the hub to the center lines of two holes. This American Classic front hub has a 42 mm diameter.

It's important to be as accurate as possible. On the other hand, unless you're using a radial lacing pattern, a slight error in measuring won't matter much. Try to stay within 1 mm.

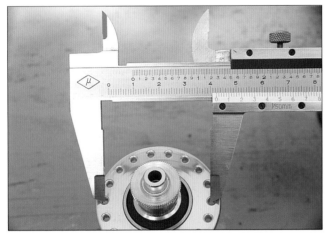

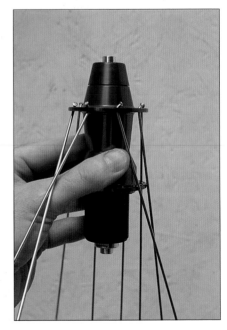

Wheel Building (photos 5-11 through 5-22)

Photo 5-11

If you're building a rear wheel, sort your spokes into two piles by length: long for the left side and short for the drive side. Begin with the hub held vertically. If it's a rear hub, the drive side should point down. From above, drop one spoke through every other hole of the upper flange.

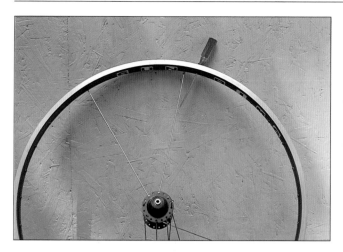

Photo 5-12

Support the rim horizontally on the workbench with the valve hole facing away from you. Put a nipple in the first hole to the left of the valve hole and attach a spoke to it. (Throughout these instructions, a screwdriver will be inserted through the valve hole when necessary to indicate its position.) Now move counterclockwise and drop a nipple in the fourth hole. There should be three empty holes between your first spoke and this nipple. Attach a spoke to this nipple.

For now, thread the nipples down onto the spokes until two or three threads remain visible.

Photo 5-13

Continue counterclockwise around the rim, inserting a nipple and attaching a spoke in every fourth hole. When you've finished, rotate the hub counterclockwise so that the spokes slant away from the holes in the rim. In this photo, the drive side is facing away from you.

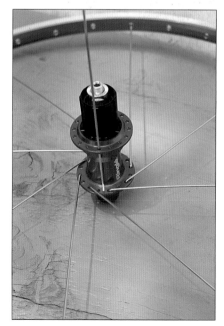

Photo 5-14

Turn the wheel over. Sight down from what is now the upper flange to the lower flange. Note that holes in the upper flange do not exactly align with the holes in the lower flange, but that a spoke dropped through an upper hole falls between two lower holes.

pawls, that transfer all your pedaling energy to the wheel. It's the pawls you hear clicking when you coast. Some manufacturers use two pawls, some use three. Some have abandoned pawls in favor of ratcheting mechanisms or some type of Sprague clutch.

Pawls are the Achilles' heel of hubs and account for most hub failure. (Second most common cause: cracks around the spoke holes.) Some riders even brag about how many hubs they've broken. They think it's indicative of their incredible strength. More likely, it's indicative of their poor coordination and abusive riding style.

Modern hubs — especially mountain bike models — are nearly indestructible. Still, if you're building a tandem or have another reason to be concerned about the longevity of your rear hub, find a heavy-duty model with a good reputation for durability.

Spokes

Spokes also come anodized in a variety of colors and multicolors. The most common spoke material is stainless steel; it strikes an excellent balance between strength, weight, and cost. Titanium spokes have become more popular, and spokes made of exotic materials, such as carbon fiber, are usually available from someone somewhere.

Manufacturers of traditional spokes have used design and technology to reduce some of the ways spokes hinder performance. Bladed spokes have flattened cross sections. The idea is to provide for laminar air flow and to reduce turbulence. Coast-down tests suggest there is an advantage. If you select bladed spokes, make sure the hub you choose is compatible with them.

Butted spokes reduce weight. They are thicker on the ends than in the middle. The variation in thickness matches the variation in stress levels within the spoke. Weight can also be reduced with the use of alloy nipples.

Spoke diameters used to be given in gauges, with 14 and 15 gauge most common. You can still order them that way, but the packages will come marked with the International Standards Organization (ISO) dimensions of 2.0 mm and 1.8 mm, respectively. (With wire gauge, the lower the number, the thicker the spoke.)

Tools   First on the list is a truing stand. It is possible to true a wheel on the bike, using the fork legs, seatstays, or cantilever brake bosses as guides. But that's impractical. Homeowner-quality truing stands aren't expensive, they last forever, and store in little space. They're also more precise than improvised tools, especially for radial runout ("hop").

Second on the list is a dishing tool. Everything said about homeowner-quality truing stands applies here too. If you choose not to use the tool, you can get adequate results by laying the rim on a flat surface, pushing one side down, and measuring the rise on the other side. Flip the wheel over and repeat the procedure. The two dimensions must be equal.

Dish is the amount of hub flange offset from one side of the wheel to the other. Front wheel dish is zero. For the back, the side with the drive mechanism is dished to accommodate it. In other words, the hub ends of the spokes on the drive side are nearer the hub's center and farther from the locknut than those on the other side. Dishing is required to keep the center of the rim aligned with the center of the hub.

Third on the list of tools is a spoke wrench. Find one that's comfortable in your hand and fits the nipples snugly; that usually rules out the one-size-fits-all variety.

Optional Tools and Equipment

Spoke compound isn't necessary, but it is worth the minimal cost. It forms a light bond after it dries to keep spokes from working loose. It also makes for easier truing in the future by preventing galvanic welding of the spokes and nipples.

A Wheelsmith spoke tensiometer ensures that all spokes are properly tensioned. It helps the mechanic, especially the inexperienced mechanic, build a set of nearly perfect wheels. The tool is too expensive to justify if you're building just one pair of wheels. But if you know you'll be building other wheels in the future, the cost per use begins to make sense.

Tensioning wheels without a tensiometer is trickier but not impossible. Start with a visit to a bike shop. Find a wheel similar to the one you're building: one with similar hub and rim, and spokes of the same gauge you're using.

Grab the spokes and note the amount of flex. Note the difference between front and rear wheels, and between the left and right sides of the rear wheel. (Both sides of the front wheel should feel the same.) Spin the wheel while holding a screwdriver lightly against the spokes. Listen to the "ping" the spokes produce. Try to replicate the tension and pitch in your wheel.

Photo 5-15

Find the hole in the upper flange that is immediately to the right of the original spoke in the lower flange. Drop a spoke through that hole. Skip one hole and drop another spoke. Continue around the hub in this way until every other hole in the upper flange has a spoke.

Drop a nipple through the first hole to the right of the original nipple in the rim; that is, this nipple will be in the second hole to the right of the valve hole. Attach the first spoke you dropped through the upper flange to this spoke.

Photo 5-16

Continue clockwise around the rim, inserting a nipple into every fourth hole and attaching the next spoke to it. In this photo, the drive side is facing toward you.

Now drop a spoke through each remaining hole in the bottom flange. This is the flange you started with — the non-drive side, if it's a rear wheel. The heads of these spokes will be on the inside of the flange, where the heads of the original group were on the outside.

Next you'll flip the wheel again. Stop when it's vertical, and manipulate the spokes you just inserted so that they lie flat. Don't force them; work them around until their elbows are oriented such that the spokes lie flat. This will keep them from falling back out of the holes when the wheel is turned over. Once the spokes are in position, turn the wheel over the rest of the way.

Note that the first group of spokes in this flange run to the right. For a three-cross pattern, each spoke in this second group will run to the left.

Take any spoke in this group and pull it to the left over the next two adjacent spokes, then under the third spoke. Drop a nipple through the first available hole and attach the spoke to it. Continue this way around the rim, doing each spoke in succession.

Threading these spokes under another will require that you bend them slightly. This is normal, and won't hurt the spoke as long as you bend only as much as is necessary to put it in place.

You'll also note that the spokes feel stiff as you thread them onto their nipples. This is because the spokes are not yet aligned properly with the nipples. As you tension the spokes and true the wheel, the spokes will settle into their correct position.

Drop a spoke through each of the remaining holes in what is now the lower flange. Flip the wheel over as you did earlier, making sure the spokes lie flat.

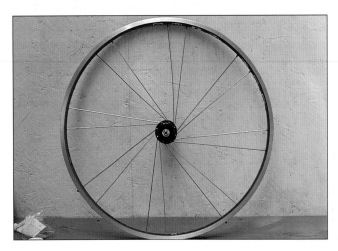

Photo 5-17

Lace this final set of spokes as you did the third set. Your wheel will look like the one in this photo when you're finished.

You can begin the truing process now by going around the rim and tightening each spoke one turn at a time. Stop when you begin to feel tension. In many instances, this occurs when the last thread of the spoke is just obscured by the nipple. All spokes should now be equally far into their nipples.

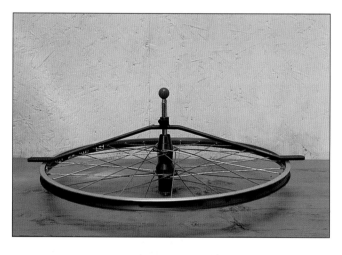

Photos 5-18 and 5-19

Check the wheel now to get some sense of how much it's dished. It's a good idea to check several places on the wheel to be sure a high or low spot isn't giving a false indication of the amount of dish.

When the finished wheel is dished correctly, the center of the dishing tool will rest against the locknut, and the arms of the tool will rest on the rim; this should be the same for both sides. Strive for a hub that's centered exactly. In any case, the deviation should be no more than 2 mm.

Note that in the photo in the center of the page [the one with the gear side facing down], the dishing tool is flush against the locknut, whereas in the photo below, the dishing tool is above the locknut. This shows that the hub must be pulled to the drive side in order to be centered relative to the rim.

To do this, you need to tighten the spokes on the opposite side; in this case, it would be the non-drive side. Turn each nipple on that side one-half turn, and check the dish again.

Once you have the initial dish, you can continue to true the wheel. Check the dish periodically, after every third or fourth round of spoke tightening, to make sure it's still correct. If not, make corrections as above.

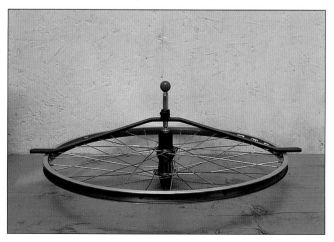

At the very least, use the screwdriver method to tension your spokes. Consistent tension is more important than optimal tension. Listen for spokes that are lower or higher pitch than the others. A lower pitch means they are too loose; a higher pitch, too tight.

One last optional tool is the spoke driver, which speeds up the initial installation of nipples. It turns the heads of the spokes from inside the rim. A ¼ in. flat-blade screwdriver works nearly as well.

If you're using deep-section aero rims, you'll have trouble holding a nipple in place while you start threading a spoke into it. The tool to use here is another spoke. Thread the nipple, head first, a few turns onto this spoke, and use the spoke to hold the nipple in place.

Tires

Tire width affects rim choice, as we've already discussed. What else do you look for in a tire?

That depends on your priorities. I once bought a new bike with wonderful tires — light, responsive, fast. But in my part of the country they use cinders from the electrical power plant on the roads in winter. Cinders are like tiny shark's teeth. Those tires were no match for the cinders. On one spring ride, I flatted four times in 19 miles. After exhausting my supply of tubes and patches, I had to call my wife to come pick me up.

I switched to Kevlar-belted tires and cut my flats by 95 percent. The Kevlar tires were heavier, but otherwise performed much like the stock rubber: a worthwhile trade.

Not all Kevlar-belted tires are created equal, however. Some have a narrow strip of the material in the center of the tread. Others have a band that covers the tire from bead to bead.

What other qualities should you consider? Comfort. Traction. Weight. Rolling resistance. Cornering ability. Kevlar bead versus steel bead (i.e. weight and foldability). Tire construction has been infused with a flood of technology over the past decade. Check the sales literature to find out what features are available.

It's true there are good road tires and there are great road tires, but there are very few poor road tires; most models are up to the demands of most riders.

The same can't be said for mountain bike tires. Since mountain bike tires have become more function-specific, the risk of getting the wrong tire has increased. A model that works well on hardpack will likely leave you stuck in wet conditions. Manufacturers' recommendations aren't always reliable, either. The best bet is to ask other riders about their experiences.

What else? I've had excellent results using Velox cloth rim strips. They outlast a dozen rubber or plastic strips.

Despite product development of latex tubes, butyl tubes are still more durable. Whether you're willing to pay the weight penalty is your call.

Presta valves are light and easier to inflate. But if you ride through rural areas devoid of bike shops, you're unlikely to find presta tubes anywhere. Tubes with Schrader valves, however, will be on the shelves of every hardware and farm supply store you encounter.

Quick Releases

Quick releases (QRs) have two functions: to hold the wheel securely in place, and to release it quickly (hence the name) when necessary. From this simple concept have sprung 10,000 design iterations.

If you're a QR manufacturer, how do you distinguish your product from the other 9,999 out there? How many performance claims can you make for such a simple device?

Darn few. That's why QRs are often marketed on other aspects. They come anodized. They come in titanium. They come with laser etching and cutout handles and contrasting lettering. They come cheap and they come dear. And they all do just two things: hold the wheel most of the time, and release it at others.

The important thing is that you know how to use them. It's not that they're so complex, it's that the cost of error is so high. Having a wheel drop off while you're airborne is exciting. Landing without that wheel, however, is no kind of fun. Read the information that comes with the QRs you select so you know how they operate.

Having said all that, I'll mention that flashy QRs are a great way to dress up your bike. If you want to spring a few extra dollars for some panache, here's the place to do it.

They're Gorgeous — Now What?

Look at the wheels you've built. Beautiful, aren't they? It's easy to see why there's a sense of awe, a feeling of magic about building wheels. You're your own Merlin now.

Once your wheels are built, you're ready to move on to the next phase: the drivetrain.

Photos 5-20 and 5-21

The Wheelsmith spoke tensiometer attaches to a single spoke about midway between the nipple and the first cross (photo on left). The deflection of the spoke is translated to a value on a scale on the end of the tool (photo on right). The instructions include an index that gives the correct value for various types of spokes.

Without a tensiometer, you can use the methods described earlier in the text to compare your wheel to a factory-built or professionally built wheel. Again, optimum tension is important, but equal tension is more important.

When all spokes have equal tension, the wheel may be badly out of true. In the end, the trued wheel will not have identical spoke tension throughout. But the tensions will be close, and they will all fall within a narrow range of acceptable tension.

Photo 5-22

After checking the dish for the first time, help the spokes bed in before continuing the truing process. Do this by first pushing down on the spokes where they exit the hub to make sure the elbows lie flat. Then grab one pair of spokes from one side of the hub and their opposing pair from the other side, and squeeze them together to prestress them.

Continue truing the wheel by turning the nipples no more than one-half turn at a time. As the wheel becomes more true, you'll work in smaller increments; even one-eighth of a turn will produce noticeable results. Check tension and dish, and prestress the spokes periodically.

The finished wheel should have no more than a millimeter of lateral (side-to-side) runout, and no more than 2 mm of radial (in-and-out) runout.

The final check should involve, in this order: dish, prestress, tension, runout.

Photo 5-23

The Shimano Nexus is one of a new breed of internally geared hubs. (Sachs and Sturmey-Archer also make them.) Available with anything from 2 to 7 speeds (with 9- and 12-speed varieties in the works), internally geared hubs are strong enough for all but the most rigorous demands. They're ideally suited for city bikes. Although heavy, they replace a number of other components, so the net weight gain is less than it would seem at first.

Photo 5-24

Unless you're using a nutted axle, the final component in building a wheel will be the quick release. These QRs from Salsa, Ringlé, and Kore save a little weight and look great. The important thing is, they keep your wheels securely on the bike until you need to remove them.

Photo 5-25

The three-cross pattern is most common. It's so named because each spoke crosses three others. Each fingertip in this photo points to one of those crossing points. Note that one is right next to the hub, one only a little way from it, and the third slightly farther out.

Chapter 6

Drivetrain and Brakes

Now we move on to the system that makes your bike go, and the system that makes it stop. Once again, light weight and durability are the watchwords for manufacturers of these parts. Rigidity takes on new importance, however. Controlled flex is desirable in wheels, frames, even handlebars. But drivetrain and brake components must be rigid.

The best drivetrain performance is realized by using parts from one manufacturer, preferably from one group. Problems can arise when mixing and matching pieces. Some components are more likely to introduce trouble than others. A list of parts in order from most sensitive to least would be: derailleurs, cog sets, chainrings, chain, and crankset.

Brakes are generally less sensitive to interbrand marriages. And though road brakes work best with road levers, and mountain brakes with mountain levers, they can be intermixed. The Mikkelsen touring bike, for example, uses Shimano STI road levers and cantilever brakes.

The Drivetrain

Think of the drivetrain as two separate assemblies connected by a third. In front, there's a bottom bracket, crankset, chainrings, and derailleur. In back, there's a derailleur and cog set. Connecting the two is a chain.

It's important to keep this entire assembly in mind from the moment you begin designing your bike. The alignment of the chainrings with the rear cogs is critical, and relies on the size and style of bottom bracket, the frame design, the bottom bracket shell width, and the spider (the usually 5-legged part to which the chainrings mount).

The goal is a middle chainring of a triple crankset that is directly in line with the middle cog of a 7- or 9-speed cog set, or in line with the space between the fourth and fifth cog of an 8-speed cog set. With double chainrings, the space between the two rings should line up the way the middle ring of a triple does.

Selecting a Bottom Bracket First a note of caution. Installing a bottom bracket, like installing a headset, is an excellent opportunity to damage or even ruin your frame. Proceed slowly, use a gentle touch, and make sure the threads are cleaned and greased.

Be especially wary of cross-threading the bottom bracket; its threads are fine and it's easy to do. If it happens, back out the bottom bracket and try to repair the shell. (The shell is usually the softer material and is therefore more likely to be damaged.) Use a wire brush, jeweler's file, dental pick, or similar tool to straighten out the threads. If that fails, you'll have to have new threads cut.

Some bottom brackets allow limited side-to-side adjustment; 4 to 5 mm is typical. The biggest factor in achieving proper alignment is getting the correct spindle length.

It's also important that the spindle be installed correctly. Normally, one side is longer from the tip to where the shoulder for the bearings is located. This is the drive side. Another way to check is to look at the emblem or printing (if any) on the spindle. It should read left to right when viewed from the riding position.

Discuss your ideas with the frame builder and with the bottom bracket and crankset manufacturers. You'll need to know three things. First, the shell width, which is usually 68 mm, but may be 73 mm. Second, the spindle length. An average length is 113 to 115 mm, although other common sizes run from 110 to 122 mm. Triple chainrings require longer spindles to maintain clearance between the inner ring and the chainstays. The third thing is thread type. Most frames use English threads; Italian threading is often available if you request it.

Manufacturers can trim weight off their bottom brackets by using alloy and titanium parts. If the bottom bracket you choose has titanium bolts, don't use them to tighten the crank arms. Install the arms first with steel bolts tightening them fully, then remove the steel bolts and replace them with the titanium ones. Otherwise, you may strip the threads from the titanium bolts.

Selecting a Crankset The first step in choosing a crankset is deciding whether to use a double or a triple chainring. Except for road racing models, most bikes now have triple rings. Triples offer a wide range of gearing while retaining small incremental changes (jumps) from one gear to the next. Triples are now available in quality road groups as well.

The next step is to select between standard and compact drive. The advantages of compact styles include reduced weight and greater ground clearance. The main disadvantage is accelerated

Photo 6-1

Left to right: Bottom brackets from White Industries, Shimano, American Classic, Grafton, and Sachs.

The White Industries model provides a wide range of adjustability; its position is held with set screws. It's installed with a standard bottom bracket wrench. The Shimano XTR model is installed with a cartridge bottom bracket tool. The American Classic requires a special tool that looks like a hex nut. The tool is supplied with the purchase of the bottom bracket. The red anodized Grafton installs with a pin spanner and bottom bracket wrench. The Sachs requires a special wrench that fits the six fluted insets on the collar.

Photo 6-2

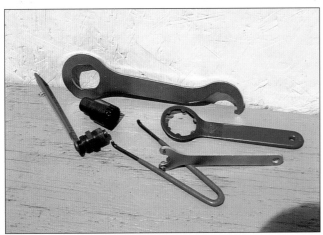

In the back is a Sugino bottom bracket tool. The enclosed end installs and removes right-side cups. The hooked end tightens the lockring on left-side cups. The left-side cup itself is held in place while the lockring is tightened with a pin spanner.

The red-handled, adjustable model in the center is from Park. A fixed model is on top of it. The Park tool with the blue handle and six teeth installs bottom brackets such as the one provided by Sachs used on the SoftRide. The black tool in front of the Sugino wrench installs and removes Shimano cartridge-type bottom brackets. The tool can be turned with a box or open-end wrench or with a ⅜ in. drive ratchet. To the extreme left is a crank extractor. The larger threads mate with threads inside the crank-arm hole. Once those threads are completely engaged, the handle is turned clockwise, driving a center bolt against the spindle, forcing the crank arm off of it.

Photo 6-3

If the frame was properly prepped after it was built, you shouldn't have to do anything to the bottom bracket threads. If the threads are damaged or have welding slag or other debris, contact the builder — or do it yourself.

The Park kit to cut bottom bracket threads consists of a left and right tap, a die to square up the face, a pilot rod to keep the two taps in alignment, and a bottle of cutting oil. The same equipment is used to clean up dirty or damaged threads, or to condition threads (chase) prior to installation of the bottom bracket. The SoftRide and Crosstrac frames came with the bottom bracket perfectly finished. This photo was taken only to illustrate how the tool works.

Photo 6-4

The tool is put in place with the pilot rod connecting the left and right halves.

Photo 6-5 (center)

Once the threads are cut, the facing die is attached. It's used to square up the bottom bracket face and remove paint.

Photos 6-6 and 6-7 (below)
Here the tool is fully inserted into the Crosstrac frame (left). On the right, the cutter is shown removing a slight amount of material from the bottom bracket shell.

Once the threads have been chased, or as your first step if the builder did the chasing, clean them with a stiff bristle brush. A toothbrush works well. Also clean the threads on the bottom bracket.

If the bottom bracket you've selected fits entirely within the bottom bracket shell, the shell needs no further prep work. If the bottom bracket is of the type where parts of it come in contact with the face of the shell, you'll need to remove any paint from that face. Use a fine file and the same technique you used for facing the head tube prior to installing the headset.

After facing, clean the threads again, then give them a liberal coat of waterproof grease. Try threading the bottom bracket in gently by hand. If it doesn't go, check the threads again.

Remember that English-threaded bottom brackets have left-hand threads on the right (drive) side; the right-side cup is installed by turning it counterclockwise.

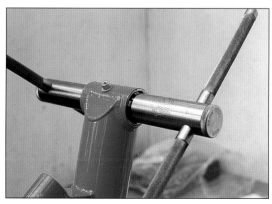

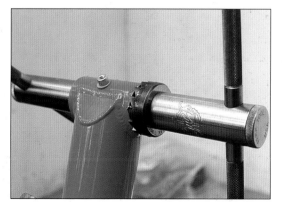

wear on the chain, cogs, and rings. Another is that if you're used to spinning big gears, compact drive may not offer enough gear-inches for you.

Three figures are important when selecting a crankset. First is crank-arm length. Common sizes are 165, 170, 172.5, and 175 mm. Shorter riders require shorter crank arms to achieve correct bike fit. Road riders use shorter cranks because these riders' cadence (pedaling speed) is generally higher. Mountain bikers use longer cranks because they provide more leverage. Some suggested sizes are given in Table 6-1.

The second figure in selecting a crank is Q factor. This is the distance between the pedal end of the crank and the center line of the bicycle. Opinions vary on the importance of selecting the correct Q factor and on the method for doing so. If it matters to you, try to match the Q factor with the width of your hips. (Measure your hips at the greater trochanter, because it's these joints, not the muscle and fat that cover them, that are affected by Q factor.)

The third figure is chainring bolt spacing. This figure matters mostly because it dictates the selection of chainrings and, therefore, the gearing of your bike. Future availability of rings should be good with standard road cranks, and with standard and compact mountain bike cranks.

Some cranks have the spider fixed to the crank arms. Others have an interchangeable spider, which allows the same crank to be used with either compact or standard drive chainrings.

Bolt spacing is measured two ways. The first measure, bolt circle diameter, is the distance from one hole through the center of the ring to the other side. The second, hole center to hole center, is

Table 6-1 Crank Length

Rider Height	Application	Crank Length (mm)
under 5' 6"	Road	165
under 5' 6"	MTB	165
5' 6" to 5' 10"	Road	170
5' 6" to 5' 10"	MTB	172.5 or 175
5' 10" to 6' 2"	Road	172.5 or 175
5' 10" to 6' 2"	MTB	175 or 180
over 6' 2"	Road	175
over 6' 2"	MTB	180

Table 6-2 Chainring Bolt Pattern Dimensions

Chainring	Bolt Circle Dia. (mm)	Center-to-Center (mm)
std. triple inner	74	43.5
std. triple middle, outer	110	64.7
compact inner	58	34.1
compact middle, outer	94	55.3
double (road)	130	76.4

Table 6-3 Typical Highest and Lowest Gear in Inches

Application	Chainring	Cog	Low Gear	High Gear
Road (700C)	39–53	12–28	38	119
MTB (26-in)	24–52	12–32	20	114

measured between the centers of two adjacent bolt holes—see Table 6-2.

The chainring size is expressed in number of teeth and is used to compute gear-inches. The others are cog size (also in number of teeth) and rear wheel size (in inches). Divide the chainring size by the cog size and multiply by the rear wheel diameter in inches. For example, a 53-tooth chainring, a 12-tooth cog, and a 27 in. wheel would yield 119 gear-inches. This would typically be the highest gear on a road bike. Common gear-inch ranges are given in Table 6-3.

One final note regarding crank selection: some manufacturers drill blind holes for pedals; that is, the hole doesn't go all the way through the crank arm. In theory, this makes the arm stiffer. In practice, it means a loose pedal requires a pedal wrench, which you're not likely to have with you on a ride.

A through-hole permits the pedal to be tightened with just an Allen wrench, which you should have with you. (This is assuming the pedal spindle has the proper recess in it for an Allen wrench.)

Selecting a Front Derailleur
The first thing to consider when selecting a front derailleur is whether you're using double or triple chainrings. Also important is whether you're using a compact or standard drive. The radii of the derailleur's cages vary according to drive type.

Maximum capacity is the greatest difference between large and small chainrings the derailleur will accommodate. Typical values are 14 to 26 teeth. Some derailleurs also list a minimum capacity, which is typically 8 to 10 teeth.

Next consider the mounting method, either braze-on or clamp. If the derailleur is to be clamped in place — the more common method — you'll need to know the diameter of the tube to which it's attached (usually the seat tube).

Also important is cable routing. Bottom-pull derailleurs require cables that come down the downtube and then up from under the bottom bracket. Top-pull models use cables that are routed along the top tube then down the seat tube.

Selecting a Cog Set and Rear Derailleur
The cog set will be either a 7-, 8-, or 9-speed. Some hubs accept more than one style by using shims. Be sure your hub and cog set are compatible not only for the number of cogs but also for the manufacturer. Shimano and Campagnolo require different splines on the hub.

Photos 6-8 (top), **6-9** (center left), **6-10** (center right)

Bottom brackets are held in place with some sort of lockring or other mechanism. The American Classics bottom bracket (top) has its lockring tightened with a Park wrench while the cup is held in position using a wrench on the tool American Classics provided.

The White Industries model is installed with a standard bottom bracket wrench (center left), and is retained with tiny set screws threaded through these holes (center right).

Adjustment is correct when there is no discernible play in the spindle, yet it rotates freely with no grinding or rumbling. Attaching the crank arm on the side opposite the adjustable cup and using the arm for leverage will help you check for slop.

Sometimes, holding the cup still while tightening the lockring is all but impos-

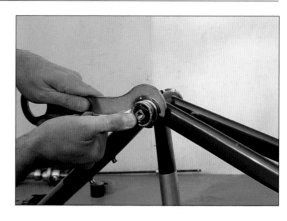

sible. Because even a few degrees of rotation on the cup can alter the adjustment, getting the exact adjustment can be elusive. Try for exactly the right adjustment, but if you can't get it, it's better to go slightly — very slightly — too tight than to leave the bottom bracket too loose.

Photo 6-11

Left to right: Mountain bike cranksets from Grafton, White Industries, Shimano, and Cook Brothers. The Grafton and Shimano cranks have spiders for compact drive rings; the White Industries and Cook Brothers are made for standard rings. In the background are rings from Real.

Photo 6-12

Here's the front part of the drive system, as defined by TNT. The XLS cranks have a separate spider so that one crank design accommodates a variety of ring types. The spider is held in place by a pocket that receives a boss on the back of the right arm. The spider is secured with three bolts. Also shown: TNT's HDS cartridge-type bottom bracket and their rings.

Photo 6-13

Left to right: Road cranks—Shimano 600 double chainring, Shimano 105 triple ring, Sachs New Success double ring. In the upper-left foreground is American Classics' mountain bike model, which is supplied without rings. It's included here to prove a point: when you get into triple cranksets, the distinction between road and mountain mostly disappears. The American Classics mountain crank would make an excellent choice for any road or touring bike.

Photo 6-14 (btm. left)
One of two critical adjustments for a front derailleur: the derailleur cage should clear the big chainring by 1 to 3 mm. Move the derailleur up or down on the seat tube (or on the lug that is brazed on to the seat tube) to adjust.

Photo 6-15 (btm. right)
The other critical adjustment: the plane of the cage must line up with the plane of the ring. Rotate the derailleur on the seat tube to adjust.

Cog sets come in several common combinations. You can also order individual cogs and build up your own. If you do this with Shimano cogs, be sure all the cogs are from the same group, indicated by the group mark stamped on the cogs. Group marks are one or two letters in upper or lower case, such as "S" (Dura Ace 8-speed) or "af" (Hyperglide-C 6-speed).

Your goal is to match the cog set to your riding preferences. Some riders want a wide range of gearing. Others want small jumps between cogs so that their cadence varies little as they shift gears. For example, Shimano's 12–28 cog set has a 15 percent average jump, whereas their 13–23 averages 10 percent.

Rear derailleurs are easier to pick than front. They all mount with a single bolt through the derailleur hanger. They all use the same cable routing. There are, however, two important considerations.

One is the derailleur's maximum cog size. This is influenced by the style of the rear dropouts, but common capacities are 28 teeth for road and 32 teeth for mountain derailleurs.

The second is total capacity. This is the difference in number of teeth between the largest and smallest chainrings added to the difference between the largest and smallest cogs. Road derailleurs commonly are rated for a 26-tooth total capacity, mountain derailleurs for 36-tooth.

A triple crankset with a 24-tooth inner and a 48-tooth outer ring, coupled with a 12–32 cog set, would require a derailleur with a maximum capacity of at least 44 teeth. No such model exists. What now?

Select the model with the longest cage you can find, which will probably have a total capacity of 36 or 38 teeth. Install it so that the chain will reach from largest cog to largest ring. (You wouldn't ride this way, but setting up the chain like this prevents damage to the derailleur should you ever accidentally shift into this combination.)

The derailleur won't have sufficient throw to keep the chain taut in the smallest ring–smallest cog combination. It may not even pull out all the slack in the smallest two cogs. But again, you wouldn't ride this way, so it shouldn't matter.

(Why not ride biggest ring–biggest cog, or smallest-smallest? This "cross-chaining" puts tremendous side loads on the chain, leading to premature chain failure. Stay in the middle of the cogs when possible, and avoid cross-chaining at all times.)

Front and rear derailleurs work best when paired with shifters from the same manufacturers. In some cases, as with Grip Shift derailleur and shifter combinations, it's essential that everything comes from the same company.

Chains Chain quality makes a big difference in performance, especially in how well your bike shifts. A quality chain has side-plate contours that mate well with the ramps and pins on cogs and chainrings. The result is crisp shifting, even under load.

Fortunately, virtually all name-brand chains are well designed. Often the only thing differentiating one make from another is the connecting system.

Shimano chains use a special pin, which must be replaced every time the chain is broken and reassembled. (*Broken* refers here not to chain failure but to intentional separation of the chain to facilitate cleaning, etc.) Assembly requires not only a chain tool but pliers to trim the special pin. The pin is a nuisance, but the design restores much of the strength where the chain is broken, which is the chain's weakest point.

Most chains don't have special pins, and can be broken and assembled with just a chain tool. Some have master links that don't require a chain tool at all.

The Brakes

We'll cover brakes for road bikes and those for mountain and touring bikes separately in the following sections.

Selecting Road Brakes Since the move to dual-pivot brakes some years ago, road brakes have all been similar in performance. They modulate well, stop quickly, and have little flex. Adjustment and pad replacement are easy. Often the only factors separating budget brakes from high-dollar stoppers are weight and finish.

This doesn't mean single-pivot brakes are inferior. Although few match the performance of dual-pivot models, they're still far better than older types. They're lighter and simpler than dual-pivot designs, and they offer a classic elegance other styles can't match.

Selecting Cantilever Brakes The bane of cantilevers has always been adjustment. Getting vertical and horizontal alignment and toe-in all just right, and then maintaining them while everything gets locked in place, has been an ordeal from the beginning. Adding to the frustration was the

Photo 6-16 (left) **and 6-17** (right)

Rear derailleur installation is straightforward; just follow the manufacturers instructions. There are some key points to remember.

First, make sure the "B" screw is clear of the dropout when you bolt on the derail-

leur. Second, the derailleur must fall in line directly below the largest and smallest cogs. Adjustment is made by turning two screws on the derailleur body; they're almost always marked. The "High" or "H" screw limits how far the derailleur moves away from the

wheel. The "Low" or "L" screw limits how far it moves toward the wheel.

Allow the derailleur's spring tension to move it all the way out, away from the wheel. Check the alignment: the derailleur's top jockey pulley should be directly under the smallest

cog. If not, adjust the "H" screw until it is.

Push the derailleur toward the wheel until it is stopped by the "L" screw. The jockey pulley should now be directly under the largest cog.

Final adjustments of the "H" and "L" screws as well as the "B" screw will be

performed after the chain is installed. Initial adjustments are done now so that a badly misadjusted derailleur doesn't overshift the chain to the inside or outside. In that case, damage may result to the spokes or the chainstay, seatstay, or dropout.

Photo 6-18 (left)

A good way to determine chain length: shift to the largest cog and largest chainring. Pull the chain taut. If the sideplates don't line up, add one link.

Wrap the chain around the top of the ring and down to about the four o'clock position. Thread the other end of the chain over the cog, through the derailleur, and pull it onto the ring from the bottom. The teeth on the chainring will hold the chain in place while you check the length.

You'd never ride cross-chained like this, but if you ever accidentally shift into this combination, this will keep you

from yanking the derailleur off the bike, damaging the derailleur and the dropout.

Photo 6-19 (right)

The small chain tool in the front is adequate for repairs during a ride. But for shop use, a quality tool is a must. This Park tool provides enough leverage to break even the most stubborn chain. It has a shelf and a stop mechanism that work to keep the pin from being pushed out entirely.

Photo 6-20

To make Sachs or Campagnolo equipment shift properly with Shimano cogs, you need to change the spacers. The stock Shimano spacers (silver) are in the upper left. The replacement spacers from Wheels Manufacturing (red) are in the upper right. The difference in each spacer is minute. But the difference added up across the cog set is significant. Without the new spacers, if the derailleur were properly adjusted at one point, it wouldn't be correct elsewhere.

The cogs are laid out in the foreground. The lockring is at the extreme left.

Photo 6-21

The screws that retain the cogs can be removed with an Allen wrench, but because they won't be used with the Wheels Manufacturing spacers, it is quicker to drill them out.

The screws aren't used because the outer lockring is sufficient to hold everything in place when the cog set is reassembled.

Photo 6-22 (left) **and 6-23** (right)

A chain whip and cassette tool ("cracker") are essential when installing or removing cassettes (left). The whip holds the cassette while the cracker is turned with a wrench to remove the lockring (right).

chore of trying to balance out return spring pressure from left to right.

The beauty of cantilevers has been in their stopping power and in that they'd open wide enough to accommodate knobbies.

Modern cantilevers stop even better and have largely overcome the adjustment nightmare. Most models now have just one or two conveniently placed bolts that secure all the adjustments without the use of ramped washers or other odd parts. Those that have individual return spring adjustments make balancing left and right return strength much easier, too.

When selecting brakes, imagine yourself performing routine maintenance, such as adjustment, pad replacement, and lubrication. If stopping power is similar among the models you're considering, ease of service may be the deciding factor.

Most brakes come with good pads, yet most could be improved by replacing the stock pads by high-performance ones. This is especially true if you ride frequently in wet conditions. The drawback to high-performance pads is accelerated wear of both the pads and the rim.

Rim wear is the drawback to all brakes that use the rim to stop. It's not a huge issue; most rims are ready for retirement by the time their walls are worn down from braking. Cracks have developed around the nipple holes, the rim has been bent beyond truing, or impact with an obstruction has dimpled the walls.

Other Brake Types Reducing rim wear was one of the goals of designers of alternative brake designs. The other was improved performance. Disk and drum brakes address both issues. Hydraulic brakes were built with only performance in mind.

Do these styles work? It depends on your needs, your philosophy, and the design you're considering.

First question: How much stopping power is enough? If your brakes can lock both wheels — not a recommended practice, by the way — they're as strong as they need to be.

Second question: Does modulation matter? A stick in the spokes will stop you *now*, but the modulation leaves much to be desired.

Third question: Do you value simplicity? Alternative brake styles are, without exception, more complicated than traditional caliper and cantilever models. You may not object to this loss of simplicity at first, but your point of view is likely to change when you need to fix a flat, service the brakes, or — shudder — replace a broken spoke.

Do these brakes have a place in cycling? Yes. Drums in particular are worthwhile on tandems. Otherwise, no. What about downhill racers? They're welcome to use disks as long as brake fade and failure don't matter. And for rear-suspension frames with peculiar brake routing? There are now several models of cantilevers, including Shimano's V-brake, that work fine.

Then why the big push for alternative brakes on mountain bikes? It's due to the migration of motorcycle engineers away from that field and into bicycles. The result has been the "motorcyclization" of this industry. It started with forks. If motorcycle-style suspension is good for bicycles, what else can we steal?

The problem with that approach is that bicycles aren't motorcycles. If a disk brake drags a little and you have a 90 horsepower motorcycle engine, the power loss is insignificant. But with a 0.3 horsepower human motor providing the oomph, the drag is a big issue.

Motorcycles have all sorts of things that aren't appropriate for bicycles. A 15 lb., No. 630 O-ring chain doesn't belong on a bicycle, and neither does a disk brake.

Someday someone may design the perfect disk brake for bicycles. It would have to be light and affordable, have zero drag, not impede other repair and maintenance procedures, resist fading, modulate well, and be simple in design, installation, and maintenance. So far, no such animal exists.

If you elect to use a disk or drum, make sure the hub you select will accept the brake. Usually that means the left side of the hub is threaded for the brake. Make sure also that the frame and the fork have the necessary fittings to mount support pieces.

Special Drivetrain Tools

The tool used to cut, align, and chase bottom bracket threads is fairly easy to use and, like all good frame tools, wonderfully precise. Like most other frame tools, it's also expensive. Quality models start at about $300 and go up to about $1,000. The results justify the procedure; the cost of the tool justifies leaving the work to someone else.

The same expensive tool that chases threads will face the shell, although facing can be accomplished with a file in the same way that you faced the head tube prior to installing the headset. If you

Photo 6-24 (top left)
The chain pin is correctly installed when there are equal amounts of pin showing on the back and front. On a Shimano HG chain, snap off the end of the special pin.

Photo 6-25 (top right)
The Shimano cable cutter works better than any other for cutting cable and housing, and for setting ferrules and end caps. The Park cone wrench is used for centering road brakes. In the back is Park's third hand tool, which holds the brakes against the rim.

Photo 6-26 (center)
The third hand tool frees up your hands to pull through and secure brake cable and adjust straddle cable height.

Photo 6-27
(bottom left)
Left to right: Road brakes: Shimano 600, Shimano 105, and Sachs New Success. Although the Sachs brakes are single-pivot instead of dual-pivot, their stopping power is on par with the best of the dual-pivot models.

Photo 6-28
(bottom right)
Road brakes mount with a single bolt. In front, the bolt goes through the fork crown, in the back through the seatstay bridge.

In the case of the Rock Shox Paris-Roubaix fork, however, a short bolt is used. A standard long fork bolt would strike the crown as the fork is compressed over bumps.

Centering road brakes usually involves holding the brake in position with a cone wrench while tightening the mounting bolt. The pads should be equidistant from the rim on both sides.

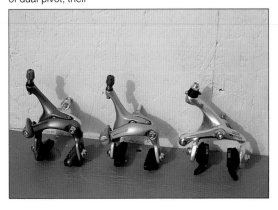

dle of the braking surface, and should make contact evenly along their length. If you wish, you can move the pads down toward the spokes slightly. Because caliper brakes move their pads up toward the tire as the pads wear, starting with the pads lower buys you a little extra time before your first brake adjustment. Be sure the pads are still fully contacting the rim, however.

Photos 6-29 (top left) **and** **6-30** (top right) Check to be sure the pads are properly aligned with the rim. They should hit squarely in the mid-

Photo 6-31

(Left to right, back row) Cantilever brakes: Grafton SC II, Paul Components Stoplights, Shimano Deore XT V-brake, and Dia-Compe VC 900. In the foreground are the Ringlé Mojo hanger (left) and Odyssey Straddle Rod (right).

These brakes represent the best ideas in cantilevers. They're powerful, fairly easy to install, and are much easier to adjust.

The Mojo hanger and Straddle Rod make the brakes feel firmer and provide better feedback to the rider, especially when used in the rear. The Straddle Rod also helps balance left and right brakes.

Photo 6-32

The only consistency among cantilevers is that they all mount on posts. Otherwise the adjustments are unique to each manufacturer.

Some installation procedures can be daunting. Don't tackle a new set of brakes until you've read all the way through the instructions. Then take your time with installation. Once you understand how to adjust pad position and spring adjustment, you'll find these new brakes are simpler than older models. It just takes patience to learn the first time.

use the tool, use it only for facing. Removing sufficient amounts of material to make the shell narrower requires a different tool.

There are bottom bracket tools you must have. Which ones? That depends on the style of bottom bracket you're using. Cartridge models need one type of tool. Traditional models with an adjustable cup and lockring need a pin spanner and a lockring spanner.

Cranks need no special installation tools. Most go in with a 14 mm bolt. But you should invest in a crank puller anyway. You'll need it eventually, and you may very well need it before your first bike is built.

Another optional crank tool that's worth the money is the little wrench that holds the slotted-head barrel nuts into which the chainring bolts are threaded. A screwdriver works, but the special tool works much better.

Derailleurs attach with standard Allen wrenches. Use a tap to clean the threads of the rear derailleur mounting bolt hole. Make sure the tap matches the thread pitch of the hole.

Installing the cogs requires a special tool. Removing them requires that same tool plus a chain whip. Buy the whip now; like the crank puller, you'll need it eventually — perhaps sooner than you think.

Except for models with true master links, chains require a chain tool. Inexpensive models are adequate for trail- or roadside repair, but for shop use, you'll appreciate the ease and precision a shop-quality chain tool affords.

Brakes install with Allen wrenches. Centering road brakes and adjusting return spring tension on cantilevers require a thin wrench. Cone wrenches are ideal for this.

Some type of third hand tool is a near-requirement when adjusting brakes. The tool holds the pads against the rim, freeing your hands for wrenching. My favorite: the sliding, locking BT-5 model from Park.

A fourth hand tool, such as Park's BT-2, is used to pull the cable taut while you tighten the clamp nut, and is somewhat less essential. You can probably get enough tension on the cable by hand, unless the cable is already trimmed too short to grab. Fourth hand tools also have an annoying habit of losing their grip on the cable. Repeatedly.

Chapter 7

Saddle, Seatpost, Stem, Handlebars, Pedals, and Controls

Selecting these parts isn't as sexy as deciding on a frame or paint; they seem downright mundane by comparison. But at the end of a 30-, 60-, or 100-mile ride, their importance will be apparent.

This is where you connect to the bike. You are supported by these pieces. Your power is transferred through them. Now is not the time to be careless or cheap.

Fit is crucial. Take your time to try different combinations until you find the one that's right for you. Getting fitted at a shop on a Fit Kit or, better yet, Mikkelsen's adjustable bike will save time and increase your odds of getting the right fit.

The Saddle

The function of a saddle is not only to provide a place for you to sit but also to enhance control. While you ride, you're constantly transmitting body english through the saddle. This is especially true when mountain biking. It's important that the saddle fit properly for both comfort and control.

First rule of thumb: the wider your hips are, the wider your saddle should be. Usually, men's racing saddles are narrow, mountain bike saddles are wide, and women's models are wider still.

Manufacturers offer not only different widths but different contours as well. Chisel-shaped noses look good, but can grab the crotch of your shorts. Some mountain bike models have the rear corners cut off at an angle to make it easier to slide off and on for steep downhills.

Second rule of thumb: saddles that are too squishy give a terrible ride. They may feel great in the store when you poke them

Photo 7-1

Left to right: The Terry women's saddle is sculpted to fit women better: it's wider, because women's hips are wider, and the surface is contoured to minimize pressure on sensitive tissue.

The Terry TFI men's racing saddle is inverted to show how cutouts in the shell relieve pressure. It's also narrower than women's models. The SDG (Speed Defies Gravity) saddle on the right is a men's racing model. The Kevlar cover is extremely durable.

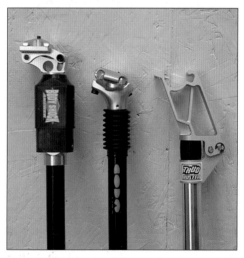

Photo 7-2

Left to right: These three suspension seatposts represent the best of their class. Answer's Body Shock post has an adjustment to remove slop from the upper and lower sliding parts. Why? Because over time, wear makes the fit between sliding parts so imprecise that they're more likely to bind than slide. A stack of four elastomers and adjustable preload provide a broad range of application. Access to the elastomers requires only a coin or large screwdriver. The post comes in one, undersized diameter (25.4 mm) with shims to fit various sizes of seat tubes.

Coda's post is a simple, straightforward design that's available from Cannondale dealers. It has one elastomer instead of Answer's four, but offers a wider range of preload. Access to the elastomer requires an 8 mm (5/16 in.) Allen wrench. This post is also available in only one size (27.2 mm); as of this writing, Cannondale was not supplying shims — you're on your own there. Coda's single clamping bolt was much more accessible than Answer's.

The ThudBuster moves the rider down and back, not up and down as do other suspension seatposts. The logic is that this motion has less effect on the rider's seat-to-pedal distance, while still offering 1 in. of travel. The post uses a single, short elastomer and offers no preload. It's available in sizes from 26.0 to 27.2 mm.

Photo 7-3

When seated in a riding position, the bump just below the rider's knee should bisect the forward pedal axle when the pedal is at the nine o'clock position. Check by dropping a plumb bob (a string with a small weight on the end works fine) from that bony bump. If the saddle is correctly adjusted and you find yourself riding on the front or back of it, don't adjust the saddle, adjust stem length.

Photo 7-4

Left to right: In the background are Salsa, Control Tech, Profile, and Shimano Dura Ace traditional stems for threaded headsets. Note the variety of extension and angle. In front: Ringle, Salsa, and Profile threadless stems. The Profile Vario is unique in that it uses a toothed clamping mechanism to allow adjustment of the angle.

Threaded stems use either a ramped expander wedge (most common) or an expander washer that flares the bottom of the stem. The Salsa, Control Tech, and Profile use the former; the Shimano, the latter.

Threadless stems use a variety of pinch bolts and cams to secure the stem to the steerer. The Ringle model shown here uses a single cam, which offers a smoother contour with no knee-gouging protrusions. The criticism is that this type of fastener can be less secure than pinch bolts. The Salsa uses a single, rear-facing pinch bolt. The Profile uses one pinch bolt on each side.

Photo 7-5 (center)

Like the seatpost, the stem should be liberally greased prior to installation to prevent galvanic corrosion. Threadless stems should be greased where they contact the steerer.

Photo 7-6
(bottom right)

Stems for threaded applications are held in place with this expander bolt, which must be tightened securely. Before tightening, check that the stem is in line with the fork and that the height is close to what the final height will be. (Large height adjustments later can cause problems with cable length.)

After the wheel and handlebars have been installed and before your first ride, check that this bolt is secure by clamping the wheel between your legs and trying to turn the handlebars. If they move, tighten the expander bolt some more.

Threadless stems have a bolt in the same place, but it's not used for the same thing. The center bolt on a threadless stem applies preload to the headset bearings. It is properly adjusted when the fork has no play in the headset, yet still turns freely. *Sutherland's* says this requires 22 inch-pounds of torque. Important: do *not* overtighten this bolt — poor handling and premature headset bearing wear and failure will result.

Height adjustments are made by moving one or more washers from one side of the stem to the other.

with your thumb, but they'll feel vague and bloated under your butt when you ride. The worst offenders are models with a half-inch of gel under the skin.

An overly firm saddle is no joy, either. Parts of you, such as your inner thigh and buttocks, can adapt. Other parts, especially your crotch, cannot.

The best models offer a compromise. They're firm where they need to be and soft elsewhere. Women's models have soft noses to prevent pressure on the labia. Men's models have soft centers to prevent pressure on the penile nerves and prostate gland. Manufacturers achieve this variation by using foam of different density, sculpted foam, cutouts in the saddle's shell, or a combination of these.

Covers are usually either leather or a synthetic material. Both have advantages and disadvantages.

Leather is durable and comfortable. It's easy to slide around on it, so you can easily reposition yourself on the bike. Unfortunately, it also retains moisture and can be hot, even if the cover is perforated.

Synthetics don't wear as well as leather, yet still give years of service — and for less money. They're cooler and, depending on the foam underneath, pass water quickly. They're less slick than leather. Kevlar is different from other synthetics. It's incredibly durable. It also has a high coefficient of friction, which makes sliding around on it almost impossible.

A word about saddles with extremely light rails. Make sure the seatpost doesn't secure the rails only at the ends of the clamp, but rather that it distributes the clamping force across a large area. Focusing the force on four spots on lightweight rails can lead to sudden, premature failure of the rails.

When mounting the saddle, make sure it's level. If it tips down, you'll be constantly sliding toward the handlebars. If it tips up, the nose will cause discomfort.

Seatposts

In seatpost sales literature, the emphasis is on materials: steel, aluminum, titanium, carbon fiber. Don't start your search there; material is the least important issue. Of much greater concern are the various dimensions, starting with diameter.

Because of the variety of tube types used in frames, there is a variety of seatpost diameters to match. Your frame and post must be an exact match; even a 0.2 mm discrepancy one way or the other renders the post unusable.

The next dimension is length. Be sure you'll have enough post above the seat cluster to provide proper ride height without exceeding the minimum insertion mark on the post. Never, *never* ride with the post extended beyond this mark.

Another length consideration concerns suspension seatposts. To accommodate the suspension mechanism, most models protrude above the seat cluster quite a bit; some have more than 3 in. showing above the cluster. Make sure that doesn't result in a saddle height that's too high.

Diameter in millimeters is always stamped on the post. Length is often also shown.

Clamps cause more frustration than any other part of a seatpost. Inaccessible bolts and finicky mechanisms can make it all but impossible to set the saddle where you want it. The situation is made worse by some saddles. If possible, try the post and the saddle together before you buy them. You won't be adjusting your saddle often, but even once is too much if it's a two-hour ordeal.

Avoid posts with clamps whose position is a radical departure from the norm. Triathlete posts and some other styles may position you too far forward or rearward for general cycling. Also see the earlier caveat regarding lightweight saddle rails and clamp designs.

No special tools are required to install a saddle or seatpost. One critical step is to grease the post before inserting it into the frame. Dissimilar metals like to swap electrons, especially in the presence of moisture, which leads to galvanic corrosion. When this occurs, it can become impossible to remove the post from the frame. Grease prevents corrosion by keeping moisture out and by forming a barrier to the electrons.

Some people erroneously believe a saddle's fore-and-aft adjustment is used to achieve proper reach to the handlebars. In fact, the stem determines the reach. The saddle is adjusted for proper positioning of the rider's feet on the pedals.

A saddle that's too low or too high results in lost power and can lead to injury. Saddle height can be measured several ways. None is exact.

The following techniques will only approximate your correct saddle height, which will vary depending on your pedaling style. For example, a rider whose toes are pointed downward at the

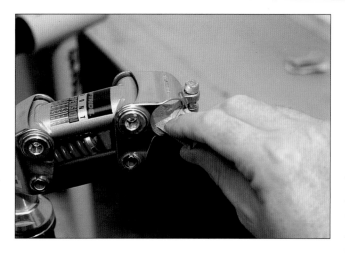

Photo 7-7

Check for burrs before installing the handle-bars. If you find any, remove them with fine sandpaper or emery cloth. Burrs will score the handlebars, causing stress risers that can lead to breakage. Lightweight bars and bars made of aluminum alloys or carbon fiber are especially sensitive to this.

Photo 7-8

If the bar clamp is threaded all the way through, you can spread the clamp by install-ing the bolt from the back side while blocking the other hole with a coin. Otherwise, try prying the clamp open with a screwdriver.

Don't force the clamp to open any wider than necessary. Installing handlebars is more like threading a maze, turning them this way and that as you try to find the combination that will allow you to slide the bars into place. Open-ing the clamp facilitates the process, but in the end, patience and persistence are the keys.

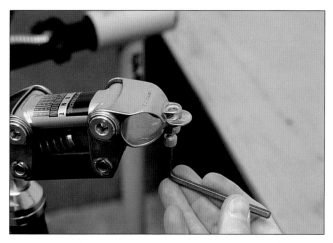

Photo 7-9

Road bars (front to back) from Terry, Scott, Salsa, and Profile. Selecting road bars is a matter of size. The bars should be about as wide as your shoulders, and the drops should fit your hands comfortably.

Note that road bars are grooved where control cables will lie. With Shimano STI, this means one groove for the brake cable, be-cause the shifting cable does not run under the handlebar tape. With Campagnolo or Sachs integrated levers, there are two grooves because both brake and shifter cables are under the wrap. Why grooves? Otherwise the cables stand up under the wrap, creating a ridge that puts pressure on your palms and fingers.

The most feature-laden bar in this group is the Terry, which not only is double grooved but also has small indentations on the back side of the drops that match up with the crotch between the thumb and first finger. These in-dentations help riders with small hands reach the levers more easily.

The Profile bar has one groove. The Salsa has two, and the Scott, none.

Note that the drops, or hooks, aren't anatomically correct. They bend away from the palm of the hand, which is flat or slightly concave. Some manufacturers, such as Modolo, flatten out the hooks to better fit the palm. Another option is to use some sort of filler.

(continued on p. 91)

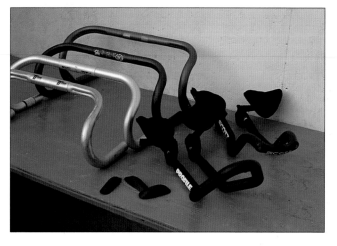

(continued from p. 90)

The Profile bar came with small metal pads to flatten the inside of the drops.

In the foreground of the photo are Ergo Grips from Off the Front. These contoured rubber pads are available in sets of three pairs of various size and shape. Put them on the inside of your bars before you tape. Do they make a difference? Absolutely. The contact between your hands and the bars is evenly distributed with the pads. Without them, the contact is focused on the edges, near the heel of the hand and the web between the thumb and forefinger.

When road bars are properly installed, they will be centered left to right in the stem clamp. Rotation is a more personal matter; traditionally, the straight part below the hooks is pointed down toward the rear wheel's axle.

On the right are aero bars from Profile (front) and Scott. They share several features: adjustable-width elbow rests, adjustable length, flip-up rests to allow access to the flat part of the bars, and elastomer suspension of the rests. The Profile accepts a Swift Shift kit, which moves downtube-mounted shift levers to the front of the aero bars.

Studies have shown that maximum aerodynamic benefit is achieved when aero bars are tilted up at around 15°. If comfort is as important to you as aero advantage, you may want the bars closer to level. In either case, practice on quiet roads until you get the hang of riding with aero bars. Even then, don't use them in heavy traffic or if you're in the midst of other cyclists during a group ride.

Photo 7-10

Mountain bike bars (front to rear) from Salsa, Profile, and Scott. The Salsa Go-Moto includes a crossover brace for additional strength in demanding conditions, such as downhill racing. The Profile Bar None bar with Boxers bar-ends is an excellent balance of price, weight, and performance. The Scott LF-X thermoplastic bar is super lightweight and virtually indestructible; it's shown with Scott bar-ends.

Mountain bike bars should also be about as wide as your shoulders. You can use a hacksaw or, better, a tubing cutter to shorten bars that are too long. But be sure doing so won't compromise the bars' strength. Some bars are butted; that is, their wall thickness varies along the length of the bar. Cutting off a thicker section will weaken the bar.

Bar-ends should feel comfortable. Ski-pole types are straight and offer only one hand position. Those with a recurve at the end provide more hand positions, but weigh more than ski-pole styles.

When installing bar-ends, try to match their angle to that of your wrist when you're in the riding position. If you use bar-ends mostly for climbing out of the saddle, use that wrist position during setup.

Be sure your bar will accept bar-ends. Some thinwall bars require reinforcing inserts to prevent bar-ends from crushing them.

Photo 7-11

Grips from Ritchey (rear) and Profile. They're comfortable but firm. They won't absorb sweat, and they provide a good grip.

bottom of the pedal stroke ("ankling") will require a higher saddle than one who rides flat-footed. Fine-tune your position by having an experienced rider ride alongside and check your leg extension. Make height adjustments incrementally, 1 cm at a time.

The first method uses your inseam measurement. Stand with your back against a wall. Wear cycling socks, and place your feet about 6 in. apart. Put a book snugly against your crotch, with one edge of the book square against the wall. Have a friend measure from the top of the book to the floor between your feet. Multiply this value by 0.883 to get saddle height.

The second method is to position one crank arm so that it continues downward along the line of the seat tube. While seated, put the heel of your foot on the pedal. The height is correct when your heel just touches the pedal with your leg straight.

The third method also starts with the crank arm extended downward. Measure the angle of your knee with your leg extended in a riding position. The angle through the knee should be 153°. In other words, the leg should be 27° short of being straight.

Stems

When selecting a stem, the first choice is whether to go with a threadless or a traditional threaded model. The decision is affected little by the fork you prefer, as most forks' steerer tubes are now available either way.

Threadless stems are lighter than traditional styles, but lack their range of height adjustability. Does it matter? How often do you adjust your stem height? Some people set the height once and never make an adjustment. Others come into the season using a higher setting, which they lower as they ride more and regain flexibility.

Once again, materials rule the sales literature. Once again, they shouldn't — dimensions should play lead roles. A stem that's too short will have the rider too upright, resulting in excessive wind drag and a sore butt. A stem that's too long will have the rider stretched out too much, causing pain in the lower back, shoulders, arms, and hands. Here are the most important stem dimensions.

First is diameter. Standards have finally evolved so that most road bikes use 1 in. and most mountain bikes use 1⅛ in. head tubes. Nonstandard sizes include 1 in. and 1¼ in. for mountain bikes, and a couple of mutations of 1 in. for road bikes.

The second dimension is length, or extension. This determines how far your handlebars are set forward. Mountain bike stems range from about 90 to 150 mm; road stems from 90 to 120 mm. If you need a stem at either extreme or, worse, outside this range, chances are your frame isn't sized properly for you.

How do you find the right length? There's a time-honored method that gives satisfactory results for most people. Start with the saddle correctly adjusted. Put an elbow against the nose of the saddle and, with the arm extended toward the handlebars, straighten out your fingers — they should fall about an inch short of the bars.

The third critical stem dimension is insertion, which is how far the stem fits into the head tube. Small frames allow little latitude here; make sure the stem you want will fit your frame. Otherwise, insertion doesn't matter much as long as the stem has the effective range of handlebar height you need.

How high should your bars be? Start with them an inch lower than your saddle. For touring, you'll want them higher; for racing, lower.

Like seatposts, stems have minimum insertion marks. Never *never* ride with the mark showing. At the least, you'll want 2 in. of stem in the head tube. Also like seatposts, stems should be greased prior to installation.

The fourth dimension is rise, expressed in degrees. A 0° rise means the stem is roughly parallel to the road when installed. (Variations exist due to frame geometry.) A –10° stem will be 10° below horizontal. A 27° stem will be 27° above horizontal.

Rise helps position the bars by raising or lowering them more than the frame would otherwise allow. It works together with extension and insertion to perfect the fit. The amount of rise, whether positive or negative, affects the extension slightly. A 120 mm stem with a 27° rise has a little less effective length than a 120 mm stem with no rise.

The fifth and final dimension doesn't affect fit but is important nonetheless. It is handlebar clamping diameter. Mountain bikes are standardized. Road bikes generally use a 26.0 mm diameter, although other sizes exist, such as 26.4 mm. Yes, 0.4 mm makes enough difference that the two sizes are incompatible.

No special tools are required for installing stems, except that some threaded models require an extra-long Allen wrench to tighten the wedge bolt. The star-fangled nut on threadless stems can be installed without special tools. But the installation is faster, more

Photo 7-12

Note that the bar-ends are well above horizontal, and the brake levers are below level. Take the time to set up your bars and controls so that they're ergonomically correct for you while you're in the riding position. Bar-ends that put your wrists at a funny angle will cause pain and numbness. Brake levers in the wrong place can slip out of your fingers or cause hand cramps.

Photo 7-13

Install the controls. Experiment to find the right location. With road bars, the brake hoods should be a continuation of the line of the tops of the bars. That's where these started. In the end, that was too high, and the controls were moved down farther into the drops. Thread the brake and shifter cables through the controls.

With mountain bike bars, controls are set as wide apart as possible. The actual distance is determined by how much room the bar-ends and grips take up. Grips can be narrowed by cutting them with a knife, but they should never be narrower than the width of your hand.

Here's the order of installation with mountain bike controls.

1. Slide on the brake levers.

2. Slide on the shifters. (If you're using Rapid Fire Plus or similar controls, these first two steps are combined.) Don't tighten the brakes or shifters yet.

3. Install the grips. A number of lubricants can be used to overcome the friction between the grips and the bars: soapy water, hairspray, window cleaner. The best is rubber lubricant, such as tire mounting lubricant. It allows the grips to slip into place when it's fresh, but holds them securely and keeps them from twisting after it sets up. Any good auto parts store should have it. (One brand name is Ru-Glide.) Leave enough room at the end of the grips for bar-ends, if you're using them. If the grips aren't open on the end, cut the ends off with a knife. You can also use a mallet to strike the ends of the grips; the ends of the bars will neatly cut the grips exactly where needed.

4. Install the bar-ends. Adjust them to the angle you think you'll want. (You can fine-tune the adjustment later.)

Now go back and tighten the shifters and brake levers. Check the position when you're on the bike, not standing beside it. Make sure both shifters and brakes are moved to the ends of the bars as much as possible.

Photo 7-14

Use electrical tape to hold everything in place while you wrap the bar, including cables and ergo pads.

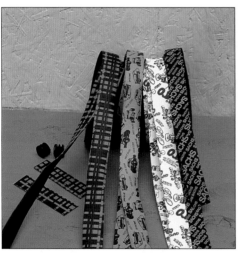

Photo 7-15

On the left is Sachs bar tape. The rest are from Off the Front. Off the Front's bar tapes are comfortable without being vague, are washable, don't have an adhesive back to leave gummy residue all over the bars when it's time to retape, and offer the widest variety of great graphics of any manufacturer.

To the right are finish tapes and bar-end plugs.

Photo 7-16

Wrapping can start at either the end or the center. Starting at the end and working to the center yields wraps that won't curl up in the drops.

Leave enough overhanging so that it can be pushed into the end of the bar and held in place with the plug when you're done.

Pull the tape taut as you go. Overlap enough so that the thickness of the tape is consistent, usually one-third to one-half the width of the tape. Watch carefully as you wrap around bends. The tape on the outside of the curve will tend to gap open while that on the inside will tend to bunch up.

accurate, and less frustrating with the available special tool, such as the TNS-1 or TNS-2 from Park.

Handlebars

Select road (drop) bars by how they fit your body. The bars should be roughly as wide as your shoulders, and the hooks should fit your hands comfortably.

Aero bars are designed to improve a rider's aerodynamic efficiency. Because drag increases exponentially with speed, aero bars can offer a considerable advantage over drops alone.

One real benefit of aero bars that gets little attention is the comfort they afford. They let a rider transfer body weight from the hands and wrists to the upper arms and shoulders through the elbows.

Considerable research has gone into the design and development of aero bars. Here's the consensus. For standard bikes, narrow elbows and a 15° uptilt provide the best aerodynamics. How narrow? As narrow as you can get without impeding your breathing. For bikes with a single, large downtube, like the SoftRide, a wider elbow spacing permits air to flow down the rider's chest and away.

The best aero bars provide adjustment in two planes. Elbow width should vary from nearly touching to 6 or 7 in. apart. Forward length adjustment should put your hands comfortably on the front of the bars when your elbows are on the pads.

Other features to look for include pads that flip up out of the way when not in use. This permits access to the flat part of the drop bars for climbing. For the same reason, look for bars with attachment points close together, near the handlebar clamp of the stem. Also, because aero bars aren't permitted for mass-start races, choose a model that detaches easily if you plan to use your bike for racing. Removal usually involves one or two bolts on each side.

After installing the bars and controls, apply tape to your road bars. Cork is the traditional material. It's comfortable and affordable, but it isn't washable and doesn't last as long as other types.

Padded tapes are washable and comfortable, last a long time, and the better ones feel much like cork. As with padded saddles, a little padding here is good, and too much is a beginner's mistake.

Some tapes have adhesive backing. Avoid them. A properly wrapped bar will not unwrap, even without adhesive, and the adhesive leaves a sticky residue that's a real pain when you retape your bars.

Mountain bike bars had curves, went straight, and now are curved again. Some curve up as they exit the stem, providing a more upright position for downhilling. Some angle back at 3° to 5° so that the wrist is at a more natural angle when the rider grips the bars. Some do both.

Like drop bars, mountain bike bars should be as wide as your shoulders. Also like drop bars, mountain bike bars have had their own accessory bars evolve. Bar-ends afford more hand positions, including a wide, ski-pole grip that helps when climbing. In extremely tight single-track riding, bar-ends are little more than brush hooks. If you ride in dense woods often, opt for plain bars or enclosed bars, such as Scott's AT-4 or AT-4 Pro.

Mountain bike bars don't get taped, but they do get grips. Again, avoid grips that are too cushy. They feel good in the store, but lead to fatigue on the trail as you continuously clench your hands to overcome the vague control they provide.

Make sure the bars you select will accept bar-ends. Some require reinforcement inserts so that the bar-ends' clamps don't crunch the tips of the bars.

With either road or mountain handlebars, be sure to plug the ends. Otherwise the tubing takes nice, circular chunks out of things: out of the paint or frame if the bike falls over. Out of your thigh or ribs if you crash.

Pedals

Few people are still using toeclips and straps. Yet there are advantages to these retro pedals. You can ride in any shoes, so you don't need to carry a second pair if you're commuting. You also don't need to invest in special cycling shoes, which can be expensive and frustrating if you have special needs (extra-wide toe box or additional arch support, for example). Clips and straps are light, simple, and cheap. They're easy to get in and out of, as long as you don't cinch the straps too tightly.

On the other hand, clips and straps sacrifice power transfer efficiency. They were designed to be used with shoes that had a cleat to engage the rear of the pedal cage. Together, the cleats and

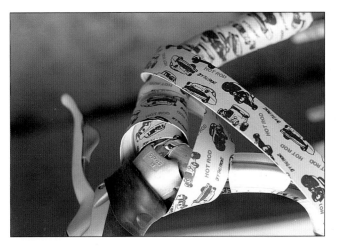

Photo 7-17

Wrap around the control levers in a figure-eight. This is a tough area. Even when the hoods are pulled back into place, it's likely you'll find little bits of bar peeking through. It may take several tries before you're satisfied.

Finish by covering the ends with finishing tape.

Photo 7-18

Whether you're installing road or mountain bars, the last step must be plugging the ends. Open bar-ends will punch holes in your body like doughnut cutters if you crash. In addition, the plugs hold the tape in place on road bars.

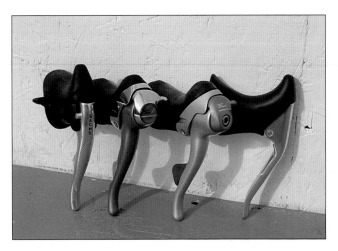

Photo 7-19

Left to right: Road controls from Sachs, Shimano (600 and 105 models), and Dia-Compe.

Like Campagnolo, Sachs uses a small lever behind the brake lever to move the chain to a bigger cog or chainring, and a small thumb-actuated lever to do the opposite. Shimano's brake lever swivels to move to a bigger cog or ring, and the second, smaller lever nestled behind the brake lever does the opposite. Dia-Compe's levers are for riders using Grip Shift, Swift Shift, or downtube shifters.

Photo 7-20

In back (left to right) are Sun Race, Grip Shift, and Shimano mountain bike controls. In front are Paul (left) and Grafton brake levers.

Sun Race provides Shimano-compatible shifting at budget prices. Grip Shift pioneered twist shifting. Shimano's Deore XT combined brake and shifter provides precise shifting and strong braking action.

Both the Paul Love Levers and Grafton Re-Entry Levers are easy to install, adjust, and maintain. They're lightweight, and the anodized finish is good looking and durable.

Photo 7-21

On the left are Ritchey WCS (World Championship Series) pedals. On the right are Shimano PD-M747. Both are competent off-road clipless designs.

Photo 7-22

Left to right: Odyssey, BeBop, and Shimano pedals (two styles).

The Odyssey Svelte pedals are for riders who prefer not to use clipless pedals, opting instead for clips and straps or Power Grips.

The BeBop pedals are extremely light due to both their minimalist design and abundant use of titanium.

Shimano's Ultegra pedals are beautifully finished, offer float, and have adjustable release tension. Their PD-M323 has a platform pedal on one side and is clipless on the other. The PD-M323 is ideal for tourists, who may wear cycling shoes all day but prefer casual shoes for dinner in the evening.

snug straps held the rider's feet firmly in place. Such shoes are all but impossible to find now.

To improve pedaling performance, many riders have switched to clipless pedals. They're available in both road and mountain styles.

Originally, the main difference between road and mountain clipless pedals was that mountain pedals had a more open design to shed mud and debris better, and road pedals had a larger pedaling platform. The former is still true, but road pedals have gotten smaller as manufacturers seek ways to save weight and improve cornering clearance.

The shoe industry has accepted Shimano's two-bolt cleat attachment pattern as an industry standard. Other pedal makers still use other configurations. Make sure your shoes match your pedals. Some shoes have a universal drilling, or come with adapter plates. These accommodate all popular cleat styles.

One drawback to the arrival of clipless pedals has been an increase in knee injuries among cyclists. To prevent this, make sure your cleats are set up properly. Additional protection against injury is provided by pedals with float, which allows your foot to move side-to-side a few degrees without disengaging from the pedal. Typical float is 3° to 10°. Some pedals' float is greater to the outside than the inside. Some offer free float, others have resistance, which may or may not be variable.

Follow the manufacturer's instructions closely when setting up your clipless pedals. Cleat position is crucial. If you tend to over- or under-pronate when you walk (look at the soles of your shoes — are they wearing evenly?), get professional help with selecting and setting up clipless pedals.

No matter what type of pedal you use, be sure the pedal spindle is directly under the first joint of your toes when your foot is on the pedal.

Controls

Integrated brake and shift levers on road bikes are heavier and far more complex than the pieces they replace. They're difficult to service, and they're expensive.

None of that matters on the road. The performance is so good, you'll never again look at a pair of downtube shifters. Best of all, that performance has made its way into more affordable entry-level models.

Shimano uses two pivoting levers, one small one tucked in behind the larger brake lever. Swing the brake lever sideways to shift to a larger cog or chainring. Swing the small lever to shift to a smaller cog or ring.

Sachs and Campagnolo use the brake lever for shifting, too. But instead of a second lever nestled behind the brake lever, they use a separate, thumb-operated lever that protrudes from the brake hood. The thumb lever moves the chain to a smaller ring or cog.

There were some performance differences between the two styles early on. The Campy models could occasionally lock up. The bugs are out of all of them now. Even the least expensive ones offer quick, reliable shifting. There's no inherent ergonomic advantage, either, as both systems seem natural after a few miles' use.

Some touring cyclists still prefer bar-end shifters. They're light and convenient to use from the drops. Some triathletes mount downtube shifters at the tips of their aero bars so that they can shift from an aero position. In either case, traditional road levers are required. Fortunately, Dia-Compe and others still make quality models.

Controls on mountain bikes have evolved, too. Thumb shifters mounted above the bars were replaced with below-the-bar shifters, such as Shimano's Rapid Fire models. These, in turn, were replaced by Grip Shift twist shifters, which were lighter, far less expensive, far simpler, and allowed the use of aftermarket brake levers.

The current state of the art is Grip Shift models that offer all the features of their predecessors, but with even better shifting. Grip Shift now has a shifter and derailleur combination; these items must be used as a system, and cannot be intermixed with other manufacturers' products.

Shimano still offers Rapid Fire–style shifters. Why? After all, twist shifters offer good performance at lower cost.

The reason: Rapid Fire Plus shifters are absolutely the slickest shifters made. Their action is so quick and smooth as to be almost intuitive. Think about shifting gears and — snick — it's done.

Index shifting and high-performance derailleurs and shifters work far better than old equipment, but are much less tolerant of poor adjustment, wear, and lazy maintenance. Pay special attention to cable adjustment; a little slack will quickly lead to missed shifts and a derailleur that hunts between cogs.

Photo 7-23

Left to right: Carnac's shoes, such as the Dune off-road model or the LeMond road model, run wider than industry norms. Still, for a rider with an exceptionally wide foot, or with any other special need, the solution is custom-built shoes such as those from Don Lamson.

Lamson's extensive fit process includes not only a tracing of the outline of your foot but also an impression of the sole. This impression is used to make the orthopedic insert that supports your foot as you ride.

Carnac shoes come with adapters to accommodate any popular cleat type, including Shimano, Look, and Time. Lamson will drill your shoes any way you want, including the universal pattern shown here.

Photo 7-24
Cleat adjustment is critical, because misadjustment can cause any number of injuries. It's best to have professional assistance in setting up your cleats, especially if you have any knee or hip problems or have ever had an overuse injury from cycling.

If you want to proceed on your own, follow the instructions that came with your pedals. Start with a neutral position, with your foot pointing straight ahead. If the pedals you've selected offer float, this neutral position may need no further refinement.

Make sure your foot is centered left to right over the pedal. Also make sure the bony protrusion that marks the first knuckle of your big toe is directly over the pedal spindle. Finally, check to confirm that both pedals are set up the same.

Control Cables High-performance cables, such as Slick Whips, make a noticeable difference in performance. Their superior sealing keeps out water and dirt better, too, which yields a longer cable life.

Make sure the cables and housings you use are properly matched. Brake cable is thicker than derailleur cable and requires a housing with a larger inside diameter. Differences also exist among brands.

Tools The only special tool needed for installing controls is a pair of cable cutters. Don't waste your time and sanity with pliers, side cutters, wire cutters, your teeth, the scissors from the kitchen drawer, or anything else. Get a quality pair of cable cutters. My experience is that the Shimano cutters work best, even better than Park's. Use them to cut cable and housing, to crimp on cable ends and ferrules. A dental pick is handy for opening up the housing liner after the housing is cut.

Chapter 8

Accessories and Finishing Touches

Your bike is virtually complete at this point. The work you do now is only a further refinement of the bike's personality.

Water Bottles and Cages

No special tools or instructions for these, the simplest of all bike accessories. Do read the frame builder's recommendations, though. For example, the Soft Ride bottle mounts require short screws. Long screws will hit the frame, popping the bonded mounts free from it.

Traditional bottles and cages aren't the only way to carry fluid. Profile makes an aero container that fits between most aero bars (it did not, however, fit the Soft Ride's Scott bars) and is ideal for triathletes. There are bottles that fit behind the saddle, in a rack pack, even on the rider's back. Most offer some aero advantage. Their real benefit is volume: a large CamelBak holds the equivalent of two and a half large water bottles. Another benefit is the freeing up of bottle cages so they can hold tool containers or batteries for lights.

Photo 8-1

Left to right: The Kage, from Profile, has an O-ring in the top groove to help retain the bottle.

The aero bottle (center) is intended to fit all aero bars, although it didn't fit the Scott bars on the Soft Ride. The black foam plug at the front keeps debris out of the bottle, while still allowing quick refills. Right behind the plug is the hole from which a plastic drinking tube protrudes. The aero bottle is intended for triathletes, although its generous size and convenient placement make it attractive for other riders as well. One problem: it's tough to thoroughly clean inside, which becomes more important if you use sports drinks instead of plain water.

The aluminum alloy anodized cage from Ringlé is light, strong, and beautiful. The mounting bolt holes are slotted so that the cage can be adjusted to provide a tight fit on bottles of slightly varying sizes.

If your frame doesn't have enough bottle mounts, these accessory containers can solve the problem. You can also have additional mounts brazed on. Some companies offer bottle cages that strap onto the frame.

Computers A basic bike computer will give trip time and distance, total distance, current and average speed, and little else. As electronic technology and miniaturization have improved, so have the available options. First was cadence, then altitude and heart rate. Now you can also track calories consumed and watts of power output, then download it all to your personal computer when you get home.

How much computer do you need? Maybe none. Some riders are blissfully unaware of any measured aspect of their trips. At the other extreme are information junkies who not only review this data but also log it for future reference.

Distance and time are nice, as is a clock. Cadence and heart rate are valuable training tools. Altitude can be of interest to anyone who rides hills, on- or off-road. If you ride at night, look into a computer with an illuminated face.

Most computers have front wheel pickup, although some offer rear wheel pickup as an option. Front wheel pickup is fine, except that it generates big loops of loose wire when suspension forks compress over bumps. The solution: wireless computers. Current models have good battery life and rarely experience interference from other computers nearby.

Installation is simple enough; follow the manufacturer's instructions. Use wire ties to hold the wire in place against the fork. A cleaner-looking option is to put a dab of silicone adhesive on the fork leg and embed the wire in it.

Nonstandard installations require a little ingenuity. Attaching the magnet to aero wheels can be done with silicone adhesive or wire ties. Fitting the computer to aero bars may require accessory parts; you may even have to resort to your own engineering skills.

To attach the Cat Eye computer to the Scott aero bars on the Soft-Ride, for example, I bought a short section of PVC pipe, notched both ends with a hacksaw, painted the pipe black, and wedged it into the extensions on the bars. The solution was cheap, secure, and effective, and positioned the computer exactly where I wanted it.

The accuracy of most functions depends on how accurately you compute the wheel diameter. You can use the charts provided with the computer or mathematically calculate the circumference from the wheel's diameter, but the most accurate method is to measure the rollout with the rider aboard.

Inflate the tires to riding pressure. Find a straight, flat area to ride on with an adjacent surface — such as a handrail or a wall — against which you can balance.

A garage is ideal. Start at one end of the floor. Mark the tire with a pencil or piece of chalk near the valve stem. Start with the mark at the bottom, and mark the floor below the tire mark.

You should be in the saddle, feet on the pedals, one hand on the handlebars and the other used for support by the wall. Assume as nearly as possible a normal riding position. Roll the bike forward. When the mark is again at the bottom, mark the floor. Measure between the two marks to determine rollout.

Most computers require metric input. If you measure rollout in inches, you'll have to convert. Multiply inches by 2.54 for centimeters or by 25.4 for millimeters.

Once you've completed the installation, give the wheel a spin. The computer should register speed. If not, the magnet and pickup are misaligned. The pickup and magnet should have marks to aid in alignment. Or the two may be too far apart. Move the pickup to achieve a gap of 1 to 3 mm. While the wheel is spinning, listen for a clicking or thupping sound that indicates the magnet is striking the pickup; move the pickup farther away.

No special tools are required for computers. Most mount with a small (no. 1) Phillips screw. A side cutter is handy for trimming wire ties.

Lights If you ride at night, in the rain, fog, or snow, or under any other low-light conditions, you must have lights. Period. No exceptions. No excuses.

Lights serve two critical functions: they help you see where you're going, and they help you be seen in traffic. Motorists aren't conditioned to look for bicycles even under ideal conditions, and almost never expect to see them at other times. It is your responsibility to make your presence known through the use of a good lighting system.

Because you're building your own bike, it won't have the Consumer Product Safety Commission's required reflectors. These can be purchased at a bike shop. You may also wish to improve your conspicuity with reflective clothing.

Photo 8-2

All of these units feature auto start-stop and mile and kilometer measurements, and adapt to fit most forks. Where noted, they have the six standard functions: current, maximum, and average speed; cumulative and trip distance; and elapsed time.

(Left to right, back row) The Sensor Dynamics SD-200 always displays current speed in the large upper display. The lower display includes the six standard functions plus time of day. The lower display can also be set to a scan mode, in which each value is displayed for five seconds. The unit's most appealing feature is Night Sight: press a button

and the face glows a soft green for three seconds. It has auto on-off that puts the unit into "sleep" mode (display is blanked) when there's no input from the wheel.

The Act C-0.5 is a bare-bones computer with only four functions: current speed, elapsed time, trip distance, and odometer. The single display is large, as are the bright yellow buttons.

At the other end of the scale is Act's C-1. It has the six standard functions plus time of day in a dual display. Speed is always shown at the bottom.

(Left to right, middle row) The Cat Eye CC-HB100 has the six standard functions plus time of day and calories con-

sumed. In addition, there's a built-in heart rate monitor with upper and lower limit alarms and a display of both current and average heart rate. This unit — and the other two Cat Eyes as well — can be set up for either auto or manual start-stop. Speed is always shown in the upper right, heart rate in the upper left, and other functions at the bottom. In sleep mode, the display shows only time of day.

The Cat Eye CC-CL200 Cordless 2 has the same features as the HB-100, including sleep mode but without the heart rate. It's cordless, which makes it a preferred choice for use with front suspension. It also stores two wheel sizes, so you can switch the computer between, say, your road and mountain bikes. (Only one mounting kit is included; others may be purchased separately.)

The Cat Eye CC-AT100 altimeter has the six basic functions, time of day, and sleep mode. In

addition, there's an altimeter — with current altitude and altitude gain or loss — plus a thermometer that reads in Celsius or Fahrenheit.

Because altitude measurement is a function of atmospheric pressure, inaccurate readings can result when pressure changes, as with an approaching weather front. To minimize this, the AT100 has a bicycle mode, which turns off the altitude gain-loss memory any time the bike is not moving. In addition, the altitude value can be corrected whenever a reliable value is available, such as at an airport.

The AT100 also has electroluminescent back lighting,

like that on the Sensor Dynamics unit.

In front is the Vetta C-500. It is wireless and has the six basic functions plus time of day. There's also a speed comparator: a (+) or (–) sign appears to the right of the speed display to show whether you're traveling above or below your average speed.

The C-500 includes a freeze-frame feature. Pressing a button saves data at that point for later review. Information continues to be updated, and the computer can be returned to normal function at any time.

Photo 8-3

Secure the wires along the fork with wire ties. Wrap excess wire around a brake or shifter cable, then attach the mounting bracket to the bars. Use a wire tie to hold the wire to the bars. This will prevent the wire from being pulled out.

Photo 8-4

Left to right: The Cygolite RAD and Cat Eye TL-LD300 both have five LEDs, offer steady and random flashing modes, and can be seen for a half mile or more, depending on conditions. The Cygolite uses two AAA batteries and comes with a seatpost mount and a belt clip. The Cat Eye requires two AA batteries and has a quick-release mounting, but no belt clip. The Cat Eye is curved to offer 180° of exposure.

The Vetta VT-20 headlight uses four AA batteries; a rechargeable NiCad battery pack is available as an option. A photosensor adjusts the light's output according to ambient light conditions, which Vetta claims increases battery life up to 50 percent. The switch has on, auto, and off positions, but no high beam.

Photo 8-5

All three of these lights offer high and low beams, have quick disconnects, and rechargeable batteries. (Chargers are included.)

The Nite Rider (left) has 12 and 20 watt lights and a remote switch. It can be mounted to the bars or onto a helmet. The bar mount includes an on-the-fly tilt adjustment. The helmet mount is especially useful for trail riding. The battery fits in a standard bottle cage. To keep the battery from flying out on rough rides, a retaining strap is included.

Nite Rider is one of the early producers of quality bicycle lighting systems, and their experience shows. Their products are nearly indestructible, offer excellent performance, and have been used in some of the most demanding conditions on earth — from the Sahara to Alaska.

The Cygolite Hilux has 10 and 20 watt lights. It's shown here with the gel cell battery. It's also available with a NiCad battery pack, which, at 2.0 lb., reduces the system's weight by a half pound. Both batteries are frame mounted. The low beam's switch is on the back of the unit; the high beam has a remote switch. Run time is a bit short: 2 hours 50 minutes on low and only 50 minutes on high (both lights on). The head swivels, but doesn't tilt once installed.

The Cygolite's beam is excellent. The pattern is good, with no dark spots or annoying stripes. The long, coiled battery cord means you can attach the battery under the seat cluster — a valuable feature on short frame sizes the clearance at the junction of the head-, top- and down tubes may be too small for a battery pack.

The Cat Eye HL-NC200 has 2.4 and 10 watt lights. Despite the low wattage, light output is very good and run time is excellent: 10 hours on low beam and 1.7 hours with both running. The NiCad battery mounts to the frame at the head tube. A rocker switch is mounted on the unit. The dual lights are independently adjustable for tilt and swivel. The low beam is a flood light; the high beam has a spot pattern.

The low wattage of this system doesn't significantly reduce its utility, but the lens quality may. It's clear the optics aren't comparable to the other two lights. There are bright and dark spots, and it's hard to get the high and low beams to overlap correctly. Still, the HL-NC200 is a good value compared to other lights in its price range.

Reflectors are not a replacement for lights, and are not adequate by themselves for night riding. Their design drawback is that they depend on incoming light to work. By the time an automobile's lights fall on you, it may be too late to avoid a collision. This is especially true at intersections, where your approach is at a right angle to the auto's direction of travel.

No savings of weight or dollars will offset the agony of a debilitating injury. Do the right thing: use lights.

Inexpensive, compact lights, such as the micro halogen model from Cat Eye, have redefined the genre. Where 18 watts was once the minimum acceptable power output for a light, the micro halogen gets acceptable performance from 2.4 watts.

You may decide a simple light is all you need. Compact models like the Cat Eye use flashlight batteries and offer adequate illumination for occasional, short-term use. If you opt for one of these, use alkaline batteries, not rechargeables. Alkaline batteries taper off slowly as they become depleted. The output from rechargeables tails off suddenly, which may leave you in the dark.

Quantity of light isn't the only issue. Quality also counts. The best lights have highly polished reflectors and precisely ground lenses. If possible, try the light before you buy. Is the beam bright with no dark spots? Is the pattern well defined?

Power Sources

There are two basic lighting designs: those powered by generator, or dynamo, and those powered by battery. Both have pros and cons, yet battery systems seem to have won widest acceptance. There are certainly more battery systems available than generator systems.

Generators provide power at any time. There's no fear of a battery running down, or of forgetting the battery at home, or of being caught out after dark without lights if you've been delayed by a mechanical problem. They're also lighter than most battery systems of equal output.

There are two disadvantages to generator systems. One is the drag they create. Even though their power output is slight, bicycle generators make lots of extra work for the rider.

The second drawback is that when the bike stops, the light stops. The generator only supplies power when it's turning.

Some manufacturers have tried to improve on basic generator systems by mounting the mechanism in the front hub or performing other design changes.

One custom shop used to offer a generator system with a small battery. You could engage the generator by flipping a lever on downhills to charge the battery; flip the lever the other way to disengage the generator and run the lights off the battery when you're pedaling. It's ingenious, effective, and weighs no more than a battery-only system. The drawback: it was available only on their bikes. Perhaps they or an aftermarket manufacturer will offer the system as a retrofit kit in the future.

The three most important considerations when selecting a battery-powered lighting system are power, run time, and configuration.

A powerful light is a requirement for off-road night rides and for touring. In an urban setting, where there's usually enough ambient light for navigation, the light's main purpose is to alert others of your presence. Is a powerful light still important? Assuming you want to be seen, the answer is yes.

Most lighting systems have both high and low beams. The low beam conserves battery life; the high beam offers greater illumination when required.

The limit on power is battery capacity. Lots of light requires lots of battery, and until technology reinvents battery design, lots of battery means lots of weight.

Dividing battery capacity by system power gives you run time. Always buy run time that offers reserve capacity. You'll need it if you're lost or if you haven't had time to fully recharge your batteries. Run time also diminishes as the temperature drops. If your system offers just enough run time in summer, you'll be riding home in the dark in late fall.

Manufacturers strive to offer the best balance of power, capacity, and run time. Variations exist. Shop around to find the system that best suits your needs.

Many lighting systems include a tail light, or you can buy a separate unit. Accessory tail lights are small and lightweight. They can be attached to a reflector mount or a seatpost, or be clipped to a jersey pocket or pannier.

Originally these tail lights flashed. A flashing light offered greater conspicuity and prolonged battery life. Then some studies suggested flashing lights actually attracted impaired (i.e., drunk) drivers, and manufacturers went with steady lights. Now some models offer both modes.

Photo 8-6

These Mt. Zéfal fenders are designed for hybrids, yet wouldn't fit the Mikkelsen touring bike. The concept is good: the fenders can be quickly removed from the bike, leaving behind only a small mounting bracket on the seatstay bridge and the fork crown. But the rear bracket wouldn't work on the Mikkelsen bridge, and the front fender wouldn't fit between the fork blades.

If the fenders would have worked, they would have been a good choice. They provide adequate coverage, and the quick-detach feature is appealing.

The Mt. Zéfal fenders would be fine for a commuting bike, but full touring fenders are better for a traditional touring bike. They mount more solidly, offer more protection from road spray, and can be easily painted to match the bike.

Photo 8-7 (center right)

The Nett Designs Load Llama is specifically designed to securely hold irregularly shaped objects. (The attorneys would probably want me to tell you that the basketball is *not* included with the rack.) Rods made of Delrin — an incredibly tough plastic — slide out and swivel, then can be locked in place. They have loops at the ends. The wide bungee net is included with the rack.

The Load Llama is ideal for commuters and others who haul briefcases, basketballs, books, and other hard-to-hold items. Nett Designs'

display at the Chicago consumer bike show had a large pizza box attached.

What's not ideal is that the Load Llama won't accept panniers. If you need bags, cross this rack off your list immediately.

Photo 8-8 (bottom left)

Blackburn's MTN-1 rack is the quintessential rear rack. It mounts to seatstay eyelets or a seatstay bridge, plus the dropout eyelets. It is strong and light, and accepts panniers. Welds are smooth. Installation is easy. The hardware includes aircraft-type locking nuts. Would this be the right rack for a trip from the Yukon to Cape Horn? Maybe not. But it's certainly up to the demands of regular touring and day-to-day use.

Photo 8-9

Blackburn's MTN front rack is the twin of its MTN-1 rear model, and the same comments apply.

Although it's shown here attached to bosses on the fork blades, the rack comes with clamps for mounting to forks without those special mounting bosses.

Photo 8-10 (center)

Blackburn's SX-1 Expedition rear rack has three supports, compared to the two on the MTN-1, making it stronger and more stable. The CL-1 custom lowriders hold front panniers closer to the ground to lower your center of gravity. Lowriders are available either with clamp or through-bolt mounting to fit forks with or without mounting bosses.

Photo 8-11
(bottom left)

Cannondale packs lots of features into a humble seat bag. There are two mesh pockets, an expandable bottom, a mount for a tail light, and a two-point attachment system.

Photo 8-12
(bottom right)

Mountainsmith Mud Puppy I and Mud Puppy III are the smallest and largest in their line of seat bags. (A Mud Puppy II, as you might expect, fills in the middle.) Like the

Cannondale, they too attach to the rails and seatpost. The mounting straps also serve as compression straps to keep the load from bouncing or rattling.

Installing Lights Investigate how the elements of the lighting system attach to your bike. For urban riding, a quick-detach feature eliminates theft. If you use aero bars or a handlebar bag, look for a light whose beam isn't obstructed by these parts.

Batteries that mount in a water bottle cage are common and convenient. The drawback is the loss of a water bottle. Some manufacturers offer batteries that attach at the junction of the head tube, downtube, and top tube, with hook-and-loop fabric. If the wires are long enough, you may be able to stash the battery in a seat bag or rack pack.

Make sure the on-off and high-low beam switches will be easy to find at night, and easy to operate with gloves on. A light with a spot for a spare bulb is a nice feature. (Always carry a spare bulb.)

No special tools are required for installing lights. Make sure when you're done that all fasteners are tight and that all wires are routed where they won't get pinched or snagged. Turn the handlebars lock to lock to make sure the wires have enough slack in both positions.

Fenders Fenders, or mudguards, keep water and road grit off of you and your bike. Full touring fenders are better at this than the shorter, sportier designs, but the sport models snap on and off in seconds. Touring fenders require eyelets on the frame and the dropouts for mounting. Any style fender is less conspicuous if it's painted to match your bike.

Racks Mass-produced racks, or carriers, are adequate for most applications. If you're going to do transcontinental touring, invest in heavier-duty, custom units.

When mounted, the racks must be level and should be centered over the wheels' axles. Stainless steel bolts are strong and won't rust. Make sure the bolts extend all the way through the eyelets and that they are secure; use a medium-strength thread locking compound. Even so, you may lose a bolt some day while you're riding; carry spares with you.

To ensure proper fit, you may want to buy your racks and bags from the same manufacturer. In any case, consider your racks and bags as a system. Will the rear rack hold the rear panniers far enough back to keep your heels from clipping them as you pedal? Is the rack wide enough to allow access to the bags with a rack pack in place? Do the bags attach and remove easily, and are they secure when you're under way?

A loaded touring bike handles very differently from other bikes. Two things about weight affect handling: how much there is, and where it's placed.

A rider's weight is distributed roughly 60 percent on the rear wheel and 40 percent on the front. Try to preserve this ratio when loaded for touring. Also keep the mass-center low by using a lowrider- type rack in front and by packing heavier items at the bottom of your panniers.

Bags The logical approach to bags, I suppose, is to categorize them by capacity.

The smallest bags fit under the saddle. They'll carry a few tools, some patches, keys, and maybe a tube. Larger models hold all that, plus some energy bars and a banana. The biggest ones often have zippers to compress them when they're not full. On the large styles especially, look for secure mounting. The best method is attachment to both the seat rails and the seatpost.

Rack packs may also be collapsible, with zippers that allow them to expand as needed. Some are simply one compartment with a zippered lid. Others have internal dividers and external pockets, including mesh pockets.

Handlebar bags have about the same volume as rack packs. Their advantage over rack packs: what they hold is accessible during a ride. Their disadvantage: they have more effect on handling, so they should hold only lightweight items.

Handlebar bags also come in standard and deluxe. The basic models are one compartment with a zippered lid. The deluxe models will have side pockets and a clear map holder on top. A desirable feature for both rack packs and handlebar bags is a quick detach, so you can carry them with you when you leave the bike.

Front panniers are next in size. Some riders consider them optional for all but the biggest tours. In reality, they're good to have on any trip. They even out weight distribution. It's also easier to find items when everything isn't crammed into two rear panniers.

Rear panniers have the biggest capacity. Some hold the equivalent of seven or eight standard rack packs on each side.

With panniers, volume is only part of the usefulness equation. Here are some other things to check out.

The bags should be rigid enough not to sag when loaded. Pay special attention to the back, the side that faces the wheel. It should be reinforced with a durable stiffener that's waterproof and

Photo 8-13

Blackburn's rack pack has a tail light mount and two zippered side compartments. The bag is insulated. A shoulder strap is included.

Photo 8-14 (center)

The Navigator Pak handlebar bag from Blackburn has a zippered pocket on one side and an insulated water bottle holder on the other. The bottle holder is removable, and underneath is a mesh pocket. A large zippered pocket on the front is ideal for holding tools. The map pocket is made of UV-stabilized material so that it won't cloud over time. On the underside of the lid are elastic straps that will hold up to four rolls of 35 mm film. In the main compartment are two zippered organizer pockets. The quick-detach mounting bracket holds the bag securely. A shoulder strap is included.

Photo 8-15 (bottom)

The Mountainsmith Summit starts as a rack pack. Off the bike it can be carried by its top handles or converted to a fanny pack in less than 30 seconds. There's also a shoulder strap. The Summit has one internal and one external pocket; neither is mesh.

A word about this and all Mountainsmith products: the company has tried to build a lot of utility into their products. For the most part, they've succeeded. In actual use, however, there's a price to be paid for all this flexibility. The Summit, for example, can be carried a number of different ways. But the confusing array of straps and buckles can be frustrating. And in all its various iterations, the Summit still lacks mesh pockets.

This is a classic case of defining your needs so you can find the right product for you. Need a versatile bag? Mountainsmith morphs into almost anything you want. Need a plain-jane bag? The dangling straps and other parts will have you searching for your scissors.

Photo 8-16

Paragon II panniers from Mountainsmith have the left and right sides permanently attached to each other. A problem? Probably not. There's no real reason ever to have just one pannier. And although the rack is blocked by the crossover piece, the piece itself has lash points for a rack pack.

In fact, the bags are littered with lash points. This is a feature other manufacturers have mostly overlooked. Too bad. When you're touring, there are all manner of things that don't seem to fit anywhere: sleeping pad, tent, sleeping bag, walking shoes, rain suit. These lash points and a few sections of rope cure the problem.

The Paragon II bags have one mesh pocket per side. There are no other pockets, either internal or external. Hand straps and a shoulder strap make carrying the bags off the bike much easier.

Photo 8-17 (center)

Switchback panniers from Mountainsmith work on the front or rear (they're shown on the front here). They have one zippered pocket per side, and no other pockets. The yellow draw cord supplies four-way compression to keep loads from shifting.

The same four-way compression is featured on Mountainsmith's Apex panniers. They also have only one pocket per side; it's internal. The manufacturer's penchant for versatility is obvious on the Apex bags: note the backpack straps. The hardware that mounts the bag to the bike rolls up and stores on the bottom, so the brackets don't dig into your back while backpacking.

Photo 8-18 (bottom)

Cannondale's Expander panniers can be used front or rear. There's an outer zippered pocket and two mesh pockets in each bag. The bottom of the bag can be zipped shut to reduce volume, as shown on the bag mounted to the bike, or it can be unzipped. The internal plastic frame helps the bags hold their shape. A tail light mounting loop is included.

lightweight. The ideal material would be DuPont's Lexan or some similar product.

Despite claims to the contrary, no panniers are absolutely waterproof. Rain covers help, as does occasional treatment with a water repellent product, such as silicone spray. The best protection is to wrap your items in plastic trash bags before packing. Boat shops carry bags that are absolutely waterproof and very durable. Unfortunately, they're also bulky and heavy.

Most bags are made from a heavy-duty nylon or similar material, such as Cordura. The performance of these materials is very similar. More important are the construction details. Do the zippers have big, rugged teeth, and are they sewn securely to the bags? Do all stress points have reinforcement? Bar tacking is the minimum; rivets are better. Is the attachment hardware well made? Will it be accessible when the bags are on the bike?

Desirable features include mesh outside pockets for damp clothes, straps to hold a pump, and several outside pockets for small items. Some models have myriad other features as well. Which are really useful items and which are useless gimmicks? The best way to find out is to take along with you everything you'll use for touring when you go shopping for bags. If you can't physically haul it all, at least take a mental picture of the items and their size. Also consider how often you'll need to get at them.

Load your goodies into the panniers. Do they all fit? Is everything accessible? Do all the bag's features have utility, or are they of less value than the sales literature suggests?

The big decision in bag design is between top- and front-opening. Each has advantages and disadvantages. For top-loaders, the good news is they're easy to fill and won't spill their contents when opened. The bad news: even with intelligent packing, you'll often discover that the item you need is at the bottom, which means everything must come out before you get to it.

Front-loaders keep things more accessible. But unless there's a good internal retention system of straps or pockets or both, half your stuff will be on the ground every time you open the bag. Front-opening bags are also more difficult to load if your style is to forcefully cram 3,000 cubic inches of gear into a 2,500 cubic inch bag.

Shakedown Your bike is now complete. The next task is to take it for a shakedown ride. Do this on a short loop so if something needs attention, you're not walking back 15 miles. And do it where traffic is light.

After the initial ride, and at least once a week thereafter, check the tightness of all fasteners, the alignment of the brake pads relative to the rims, and the trueness of spoked wheels. Check for cable stretch after the first 100 miles, or whenever performance degrades. A stretched brake cable will result in excessive lever travel. A stretched derailleur cable will result in poor shifting and the inability of the derailleur to stay in one gear.

Your perfect bike is done. Is it perfect? Is it all you hoped it would be?

Chances are you've already started mentally designing your next bike. Perhaps you've built a touring bike and want to build a mountain bike. Perhaps you want to build another touring bike, but build it differently. Perhaps what you've built now fulfills every bicycle dream you've ever had.

Whatever you do in the future, that which you've accomplished now will never lose its importance. You've designed and built your own bike, a piece of equipment that is an extension of who you are, a rolling testament to your vision, skill, and perseverance.

Feels good, doesn't it?

Photos 8-19 (top) **and 8-20** (center)

Blackburn's MTN panniers have a rigid aluminum backing plate to protect and stiffen the backs of the bags. Other features include mesh pockets, compression straps, and a shoulder strap.

A clever feature is the removable mesh bag that sits on a little shelf near the top of the bag. Ever pull into a campsite after a long day in the saddle and wish your toiletries bag wouldn't always sink to the bottom? Here's the answer.

Photo 8-21 (bottom)

Vetta's Verdict lock has an unusual shape that makes it much more convenient than a conventional U-lock when securing your front wheel. The Verdict uses round, pick-resistant keys. It's best for areas where medium security is all that's necessary.

U-locks offer good security, as do chains and cables. Using a U-lock *and* a cable is good, as few thieves carry tools to defeat both.

There are techniques for reducing the ease with which your bike can be stolen. Lock manufacturers are good sources of this information, as are more enlightened police departments.

The best security: take your bike inside with you. Lock it up in an office or closet. Never let it out of your sight if you must leave it outdoors. If you must use public parking, seek out secure spots, such as bike lockers or attended racks. The city of Minneapolis, for example, provides bicycle parking at all of its parking garages; the racks are within sight of the cashier.

Photo 8-22

I'm told there are places on earth where the gentle tinkling of a cycle bell is sufficient to alert pedestrians and motorists of a cyclist's presence. I've never ridden there.

For the places I ride, the AirZound from Sidetrak is the solution. The air canister fits in a bottle cage and can be charged up with a standard bicycle pump (it has a Schrader fitting). Maximum recommended pressure is 150 lb. A thumbwheel clamps the horn securely to the bars. Tap the button atop the horn and *everyone* is suddenly aware of your whereabouts.

It's inexpensive, lightweight, simple to operate, and effective. The only improvement that could be made would be dual tones — like Fiamm automobile horns. But even as it is, the AirZound is the best attention-getter available to cyclists.

Photo 8-23

The Vetta VP-15 and Cannondale MP201 pumps include water bottle mount brackets, reversible heads to fit presta or Schrader valves, and aluminum alloy barrels. The Vetta also has zip ties so the mounting bracket can be attached somewhere other than a water bottle braze-on. The Vetta has a locking handle to keep it from extending while you're riding.

In the past, pumps other than floor models had two problems: either they moved a small volume and would take hundreds of strokes to fill a mountain bike tire, or they couldn't muster the pressure to run a road tire up to an acceptable pressure.

These two pumps are among the many now on the market that have largely overcome these problems.

Behind the pumps are Vetta's Gryphon helmets. Like pumps, early helmets had problems. They were hot, heavy, and ugly, and often fit poorly. Improvements were soon made, but those helmets cost dearly.

Gryphons and other modern helmets have overcome all those shortcomings. One note, however: be sure to try on any helmet you're thinking of buying. Head shape matters as much as size, and some helmets can never be made to fit some heads.

One other note: some riders still consider helmets optional. That's true only if your brain is optional.

Chapter 9

Tandems

Most of the considerations given other bikes apply to tandems, too. But there are a few things unique to twofers that require some thought.

Because no special project bike could be built up specifically for this book, I have used illustrations of my editor's tandem based on a frame built by Bernie Mikkelsen and built up with a variety of typical tandem parts.

Frame　There are several styles of tandem frames. The direct lateral, with a reinforcing tube running from the head tube to the stoker's bottom bracket, is most popular. It's slightly heavier than some other styles, but it's very stiff and efficient. Talk to your builder about frame style options.

Wheels　Tandem wheels carry much more weight, often at higher speeds, than wheels on single bikes. More spokes are needed to handle these higher loads: 36 holes are the minimum, and up to 48 holes may be prudent for heavier riders on an off-road machine.

Tandem tires also bear heavier loads. Use wider tires than you would on a single bike: 28 mm is a good minimum size.

Hubs　Not all hubs are up to the demands of two powerful riders pumping in unison. Heavy-duty mountain bike hubs generally hold up best. Huegi hubs are the time-honored tandem champs, although new models from White Industries and others seem to perform at least as well.

Brakes　Cantilever brakes are recommended, but even they won't have adequate stopping power in many cases. Rather than opting for more powerful rim brakes, look into adding at least a hub brake on one of the wheels. These add more to the total braking force than merely upgrading existing brakes. They also move the heat away from the rim.

Disk brakes are OK for use on tandems, but like drum brakes, they are only suitable as additional brakes to rim brakes. The drums don't drag, they use a standard brake cable, and don't require special additions to the frame for mounting. (Either disks or drums require a special hub, however.)

The additional brake can be lever-actuated by the captain or the stoker. You can also use a mountain bike thumb shifter to set the brake as a drag brake for descents. My preference for operation of the drag brake: give the stoker control, but have the captain issue commands to "brake" and "release."

Controls The extra length from the captain's bars to the rear wheel means the derailleurs and rear brake need frequent, precise tuning to maintain performance. Much of the problem can be solved with compressionless cable housing, which doesn't deform as much under load as traditional cable housing. It's also helpful to keep the rear brake pads as near the rim as possible without dragging.

Cranks The cranks are connected with a timing chain. Some tandem teams run their cranks 90° out of phase to even out the power pulses. If you concentrate on pedaling circles, this is unnecessary. If you do run your cranks out of sync, the captain must keep the stoker's crank-arm position in mind when cornering or riding over obstacles.

Chainrings often have high and low spots. On a tandem, this can result in loose and tight cycles of the timing chain. Check the timing chain tension in several spots as you rotate the cranks, and adjust the tension at the tightest points.

This may create excessive slack at another point in the cranks' revolution. If so, remove the bolts from one ring and rotate it one bolt hole. Check the tension again. Continue rotating and checking until you find the best orientation of front to rear chainrings. (Put an indexing mark on the ring you're moving or use the manufacturer's stamp to keep track of the changes in position.)

The best solution would be to attach a chain tensioner (like those used by downhill racers) to keep the timing chain under optimum tension at all times. I'm not aware of any commercial product like this at this time. Another option would be to use the chain guides downhillers use. Either device would keep the timing chain from derailing if the bike were to hit a bump when the chain is at minimum tension.

Stoker Compartment The stoker will want a computer, too. Find one with a rear wheel pickup.

While a tandem's long wheelbase insulates the captain from most road shock, the stoker gets hammered by every bump. Part of

Photo 9-1

A direct lateral frame has a tube running from the head tube in front to the rear bottom bracket shell, bisecting the captain's seat tube. This is a popular configuration for tandem frames. It's a good compromise of weight and rigidity.

Photo 9-2 (ctr. left) Adjusting the tension on the timing chain is accomplished by loosening the front bottom bracket and rotating it on its eccentric. This frame, like many, uses two machine screws to hold the eccentric in place.

Check the chain tension in several places, as most chainrings are slightly out of round and the tension will vary as the cranks turn. Make the adjustment at the tightest spot.

Be sure when you're done that the cranks are in alignment. Loosening the eccentric allows the bottom bracket not only to rotate but also to move from side to side.

Photo 9-3 (ctr. right) Tandem crossover drivetrain detail. The synchronizing chain, connecting the front and rear cranksets, runs on the left over a set of equal-size chainrings (at least 36-tooth chainrings to assure smooth running)and the rear wheel is driven from the standard drive chain on the right. Although it's possible to jury rig something up using non-tandem parts, this is the preferred way.

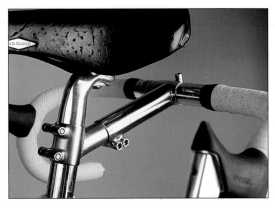

Photo 9-4 (bottom)

A good stoker compartment starts with a good stoker stem. They all slide on the captain's seatpost to provide variable height. This one also telescopes to provide variable reach.

Note:
All photos in this chapter are by Neil van der Plas

Photo 9-5

Dummy hoods provide hand rests for the stoker. If you choose, the stoker can have a functioning lever to control the third brake if your tandem is equipped with one.

Photo 9-6

This Sanshin hub is threaded for a third brake, whether disk or drum. Note the braze-on tab on the left-hand chainstay for the third brake. Note also the solid, nutted axle; tandems carry a lot of weight, and solid axles flex less and last longer than hollow axles with quick releases.

Photo 9-7

The finished tandem based on the Mikkelsen frame seen from the left-hand (or timing chain) side.

the solution is a considerate captain who avoids bumps and calls out the unavoidable ones. Most helpful is some kind of stoker suspension. A SoftRide beam works well if the frame will accommodate it without creating excessive height. Otherwise, a suspension seatpost may be the answer.

One of the joys of tandeming is the chance to ride with different people. Two components help extend the range of who can ride. Adjustable stoker stems take care of reach problems. And kiddie stoker kits move the stoker's crankset up onto the seat tube so short young legs can reach the pedals.

Tandem Touring Touring two-up is a joy. Unfortunately, a tandem doesn't offer twice the rack and pannier capacity of a single bike. If you're doing a self-contained tour and need more space, consider a trailer. Towed behind the bike, a trailer offers lots of additional storage with minimal impact on handling.

List of Suppliers

ACT USA
P.O. Box 5490
Evanston, IL 60204
(708) 491-9628

American Classic
P.O. Box 26
Canal Winchester, OH 43110
(614) 756-7900

Answer
28209 Avenue Stanford
Valencia, CA 91355
(805) 257-4411

Avid Enterprises
2875 W. Oxford Avenue #7
Englewood, CO 80110
(303) 762-9353

BeBop
8570 Hamilton Avenue
Huntington Beach, CA 92646
(714) 374-0200

Bell Helmets
P.O. Box 71932
Chicago, IL 60694-1932
(800) 456-2800

Blackburn/Bell Sports
P.O. Box 71932
Chicago, IL 60694-1932
(800) 456-2800

Cannondale
9 Brookside Place
Georgetown, CT 06829-0122
(203) 544-9800

Carnac Shoes/Sinclair Imports
2465 W. Highway 40
Verdi, NV 89439
(702) 345-0600

Cat Eye Service and Research Center
1705 - 14th Street #115
Boulder, CO 80302
(800) 522-8393

Competitive Edge
1151 E. 29th Street
Los Angeles, CA 90011
(818) 375-5020

Conix
See Competitive Edge

Control Tech
22614 - 66th Avenue S.
Kent, WA 98032-4844

Cook Brothers Racing
1983 Willow Road
Arroyo Grande, CA 93420
(805) 343-2700

Cronometro Design
2057 Winnebago Street
Madison, WI 53704
(608) 243-7760

Crosstrac/Strom Industries
1801 Mount Vernon Avenue
Pomona, CA 91768-3310
(909) 622-3554

Cygolite/SSB Design
17915-J Sky Park Circle
Irvine, CA 92714
(714) 863-1065

Dia-Compe USA Inc.
P.O. Box 798
Fletcher, NC 28732
(704) 684-3551

DT Swiss
Contact your dealer

FSA
See Competitive Edge

Grafton Performance, Inc.
463 Turner Drive
Durango, CO 810301
(970) 259-3707

Grip Shift/SRAM Corporation
1234 Carl Boulevard
Elk Grove Village, IL 60007
(312) 664-8800

J. P. Weigle Cycles
410 Town Street
East Haddam, CT 06423
(860) 873-1671

King Cycle Group
5330 Debbie Road
Santa Barbara, CA 93111
(805) 683-0950

Kore Products
11577 Slater Avenue, Unit K
Fountain Valley, CA 92708
(714) 979-5673

Lamson Design
601-C W 2nd Street
Rifle, CO 81650
(970) 625-0568

Mavic
207 Carter Drive
West Chester, PA 19382
(800) 548-2945

Mikkelsen Frame Express
2235 Clement Avenue
Alameda, CA 94501
(510) 521-9727

Mountainsmith, Inc.
18301 W. Colfax, Bldg. P
Golden, CO 80401
(303) 279-5930

Nett Designs
P.O. Box 2177
Vail, CO 81658
(800) 845-5262

Nite Rider Light Systems Inc.
8205 Ronson Road, Suite E
San Diego, CA 92111
(619) 268-9316

Odyssey/Bear Corporation
17101-G South Central Avenue
Carson, CA 90746
(310) 537-8700

Off the Front
1781 Bitterbrush
Gardnerville, NV 89410
(702) 782-2412

Park Tool Co.
3535 International Drive
St. Paul, MN 55110
(612) 490-1074

Paul Component Engineering
2574 Fair Street
Chico, CA 95928
(916) 345-4371

Profile
6600 W. Armitage Avenue
Chicago, IL 60635
(312) 237-7200

Real Product Design, Inc.
1880 S. Flatiron Court, Suite R
Boulder, CO 80301
(303) 545-9991

Ringle Components, Inc.
101 Walters Avenue
Trenton, NJ 08638
(609) 882-7800

Ritchey Design
1326 Hancock Street
Redwood City, CA 94603
(415) 368-4018

Rock Shox
401 Charcot Avenue
San Jose, CA 95131
(800) 677-7177

Sachs Bicycle Components
22445 E. La Palma Avenue
Yorba Linda, CA 92686
(800) 343-8586

Salsa
611 - 2nd Street
Petaluma, CA 94952
(800) 762-4688

Scott USA
P.O. Box 2030
Sun Valley, ID 83353
(208) 622-1000

SDG
212 Technology Building C
Irvine, CA 92718
(714) 753-9335

Sensor Dynamics
4580 Enterprise Street
Fremont, CA 94538
(800) 764-4327

Shock Works
See Competitive Edge

Shimano American Corporation
1 Holland Drive
Irvine, CA 92718-2597
(714) 951-5003

Sidetrack, Inc.
774 Industry Drive
Seattle, WA 98188-3408
(206) 575-0335

SoftRide
P.O. Box 9709
Bellingham, WA 98227
(206) 647-7420

Spinergy
45 Danbury Road
Wilton, CT 06897
(203) 762-0198

Spline Drive, Inc.
23021 Laurel Grove Circle
Lake Forest, CA 92630
(714) 588-9413

Sun Metal
P.O. Box 1508
Warsaw, IN 46581-1508
(215) 267-3281

Sun Race
2239 Poplar Street
Oakland, CA 94607
(800) SUN-RACE

Sutherland's Publications
1609 - 63rd Street
Emeryville, CA 94608
(800) 248-2510

Talon Cycles
317 E. Marilyn Avenue
Mesa, AZ 85210
(602) 898-3772

Terry Precision Bicycles
1704 Wayneport Road
Macedon, NY 14502
(800) 289-8379

Thudbuster
120 Mount Rushmore Road
Custer, SD 57730
(605) 673-3270

TnT Performance Products
21629 N. 14th Avenue
Phoenix, AZ 85027
(602) 780-4542

Vetta Sports
1500 Kearns Blvd., Suite A200
Park City, UT 84060
(800) 468-3882

Vittoria North America
1639 W. Sheridan Avenue
Oklahoma City, OK 73106
(800) 350-0688

Wheels Manufacturing
7209 Valtec Court, Suite A
Boulder, CO 80301
(303) 444-2415

Wheelsmith Fabrications, Inc.
P.O. Box 1509
Big Timber, MT 59011
(406) 932-4530

White Industries
23 Pamaron
Novato, CA 94949
(415) 382-1915

Wilderness Trail Bikes
187 E. Blithedale Avenue
Mill Valley, CA 94941
(415) 389-9050

Index